SUCCESSFULLY EVER AFTER

SUCCESSFULLY EVER AFTER

A WOMAN'S GUIDE TO CAREER HAPPINESS

by Shirley Sloan Fader
with Penny Kane

PIATKUS

© 1982, 1985 text by Shirley Sloan Fader

First published in 1985 by Judy Piatkus
(Publishers) Limited, London

British Library Cataloguing in Publication Data

Fader, Shirley Sloan
Successfully ever after.
1. Women——Employment
I. Title   II. Kane, Penny
331.4   HD6053
ISBN 0–86188–330–6

Designed by Paul Saunders

The Author is grateful to Penny Kane for her British adaptation of
the original text.

Typeset by Phoenix Photosetting, Chatham, Kent
Printed and bound by The Garden City Press Ltd, Letchworth,
Hertfordshire SG6 1JS

With love, for my daughter Susan Deborah

Contents

Introduction

Most job/career books abandon you when you need them most. They take you only up to your first day on the job. They explain valuable facts about writing a selling curriculum vitae impressing the interviewer, locating promising job openings, and so on. But once you have your job, you're on your own.

This book begins where the other books stop. This book tells you how to *succeed* during all the months and years after you land a job. Look through the chapter titles on the contents page and see how they deal with the job/career questions, problems, and anxieties you may be struggling with right now.

Yes, there are some how-to-succeed-on-the-job books. But if you've glanced through them, you know that most are written for middle-aged executives. This book has been researched and especially tailored by experienced job/career experts to meet the needs of women. It takes you from the moment you're offered a good position: 'How to tell if the job you're offered is right for you' through 'Twelve ways to make the right impression,' 'How to make more money from your job fringe benefits,' 'How to find out what other people with your job make,' 'Boss troubles and how to deal with them' –

and much, much more. Altogether twenty-nine chapters of how to cope, enjoy, and succeed.

Most important, the advice you will find in *Successfully Ever After* is practical, 'takable' advice. It's not theory; it's not fancy talk. It's advice you can read today and immediately easily *use* tomorrow – to solve your career problems and build your career success.

It was originally written for American women. We have adapted the facts and figures for Britain, but left in everything we thought was relevant. Most of the research that's going to be useful to you was, in fact, done in America. Americans are a bit more clued-up on how to succeed at work and have spent more time thinking about it. But there's no reason things should stay that way. We hope this book will give women in Britain a better chance to enjoy satisfying and successful jobs.

PART **I**

YOU'VE GOT THE JOB OFFER – NOW WHAT?

CHAPTER 1.

How to tell if the job you're offered is right for you

Only you can judge how 'good' a job is. What your friend describes as 'a very good position' might seem like a 'so-so job' to you. Why the different reactions? Different people seek different work satisfactions. In order to assess a job, you must *first* analyse your personal career goals. Once you clearly understand your own priorities, confusion melts away and you know whether the job is right for you.

Here are some important – and often conflicting – job/career goals people have. Which ones are yours? (As you go through the list, evaluate the importance of each: E = Essential to me; N = Nice to have but if necessary I could get along without it; DM = Doesn't really matter to me; C = A job like this would drive me crazy.)

1. Security. The promise of peaceful, long-term tenure.

2. Promotion possibilities. You won't be stuck for a long time. Can use this as stepping stone to promotion within your present company or elsewhere.

3. Varied, open-ended duties where you can demonstrate initiative.

12

4. Nothing open-ended. Clear routine, you know exactly what is expected of you, you're not left on your own to figure things out.

5. Constant challenge.

6. Undemanding and pleasant. You put in your time and have energy to enjoy life after hours.

7. High social content, lots of people contact.

8. People leave you alone to do your work without constant interruptions.

9. Chance to indulge your 'workaholic' tendencies. You can get ahead through all kinds of extra effort and overtime.

10. Clear time demarcations that will never make demands on your free time; no Saturday mornings, no evenings.

11. Work that really interests you. You *enjoy* each day.

12. Income is very, very important. Almost any job that provides a certain salary level would satisfy you.

13. Power. You are involved in making decisions about your own work and about other people's jobs.

14. Status. A title that impresses people during your after-hours social life.

15. Fringe benefits. Company-paid study leave; long summer vacations; comprehensive company-paid family medical insurance and the like.

16. Other. List other personal job/career goals you seek not mentioned above.

Now you know what you want: A job that satisfies your E job characteristics, has as many of your N and as few of your C as possible.

Can you fulfill your goals in your current position? If the quiz convinced you a move is necessary, how do you avoid repeating the same mistakes? After a few months elsewhere

13

will you be sighing and murmuring 'I didn't realise when I took this job . . .'?

During any successful employment interview eventually you're asked 'Do you have any questions?' That is your opportunity. Instead of inventing questions merely to appear intelligent, ask some of the following eight. *Through the answers you receive you can assess any job in terms of your priorities.* Of course, you'll have to ask only those which deal with *your* goals.

QUESTION 1

What is the nature of your job duties?

Who is your supervisor?

You cannot rely on job titles. The same title in different companies may encompass different duties and occupy different levels in the power structure. 'Could you elaborate on my job duties?' is a good question to put to the interviewer who doesn't volunteer details. Personnel *should* have a thorough job description at hand – how else will they know what to look for when interviewing you? Any time the interviewer has to waffle on this, it's a sign of a sloppy, badly run company. Keep away or in a little while you'll be saying 'This isn't what I was hired for.'

You must meet the person you will work for, preferably for a full interview or at least for a satisfactory conversation. There's such a thing as chemistry. In any job there's a personal relationship between superior and subordinate. Your success depends on your superior's attitude toward you.

Now is the time to have all your E and C criteria firmly in mind. For example, if overtime evenings or Saturdays will make it difficult for you to meet family obligations, you must extract the necessary facts. You can do this tactfully by asking 'What are the opportunities for overtime in this job?' That phrasing sounds as though extra time is no problem.

The answer may be 'Very rare' or 'Only on a volunteer basis.' You have your answer and you haven't risked prejudicing the interviewer against you as you might have if you'd stated flatly 'I can't work any overtime.'

With a supervisory job, finding out about extra hours is touchy. Executives are not supposed to clock-watch. You can often obtain some idea by asking 'How do they run the meetings?' This indicates that you know meetings are part of the job and, of course, you expect to attend. You might elicit an answer such as 'Wednesday mornings'. Or it might be 'Supervisors usually get together for dinner three or four times a month.' Either way, now you know.

When you meet your supervisor, ask the same 'What specifically are my duties?' question again. You're sure to hear new facts and nuances. Among other information, you'll find out whether this job provides social contacts or whether they leave you in relative solitude.

As your future boss describes the work, the position will basically be either closed-end or open-end. The closed-end job is repetitious. The cycle, as with payroll work, may be as long as a few weeks, but it is a cycle. The closed-end job puts a limit to the demands on your talent, your time, and your promotion potential. The open-end job is varied, often unpredictable, may make erratic time demands, and often has some promotion potential. In addition to supervisory positions, which are usually open-end, an administrative-assistant or executive-secretary job is also open-end and has some promotion potential.

The description of your duties will also tell you whether your job will have decision-making power and/or a status title. In judging these two, don't be surprised if they are *not* tied to a handsome salary. You may have to choose money *or* title *or* power. For instance, a woman who makes up sales-people's daily customer call schedules has power over the salespeople. Yet the salespeople probably make considerably more money than she does.

However, in any position previously held by a man, don't be conned into taking a title *instead* of the money. This, unfortunately, is a *very common* approach used with women employees. The woman is made to understand that since she has broken through the promotion barriers against women and now has this splendid title, she shouldn't be pushy and insist on money too. But if the man before you had *both* money and title, why shouldn't you? If you are compelled to choose, always take the money. The title costs them nothing and will follow naturally later.

If you're not anxious for heavy responsibility and want your status title for after-hours social reasons or for advancement potential in other companies, this may be easier to achieve than you think. Start with a well-known company. Where status is your priority, don't bother with other interviews. Big companies know people rejoice in titles and are usually generous with them. Besides, a medium-grade title with an important organization is more 'impressive' than a big title with a company no one ever heard of. When you're able to say 'I'm the Administrator of Employee Benefits for the XYZ Company,' people will doubtless be impressed – 'What, you have a management position with the well-known XYZ Company, *wow!*'

You may have no one working for you and your days may consist of helping employees with medical, Social Security, and pension forms and collections. But if that's the title they've dressed the job with, it sounds great. And if a status title is your E goal, you've arrived.

QUESTION 2

How long has your supervisor held the job?

Suppose the answer is 'This supervisor has held the job for six months; the previous supervisor stayed a year, the supervisor before that lasted fifteen months. None was promoted. They all just left the company.' What should your reaction be? It comes back to your goals.

The turnover indicates this is a high-pressure, difficult department. People who want a pleasant, undemanding job, security, foreseeable routine are not going to find them here. Other people who are concentrating on immediate income or six months to a year of this particular kind of experience may find the situation good.

Suppose the answer to the same question is 'The supervisor has held the job for twelve years.' Now what is your reaction? Again, it comes back to your goals.

The twelve-year supervisor, who seems dead-ended in that job, will run a department where her or his ego is affected by how the department does. Probably little chance for initiative. Depending on the supervisor's personality, it can be pleasant or full of tension. Ability will probably give you job security. Few promotion prospects. Your supervisor isn't leaving so you can't move there and she or he will fight hard to see that no one competent is promoted out of the department. She or he will want good people to stay to keep the group's and his or her reputation shiny.

Another answer to the 'Who is the supervisor?' question might reveal that the last two supervisors were promoted. Now you know the department is alive. There's upward potential for those who want it. Apparently the group is carefully monitored by the top office. This, however, can be a problem for the woman who wants an undemanding routine.

If promotion matters to you, expand this question to include 'Where does my department fit into the overall scheme?' The response gives you a quick picture of where you will be in relation to the top.

QUESTION 3

Is the job you are being offered a new job or an established job?

Is it in a new department or an established department?

A newly created job provides excellent opportunities to demonstrate initiative. You will establish the dimensions of the position, develop the routines. This job will intimidate the woman who seeks established routine, who wants to know beforehand exactly what is expected of her. The new, unstructured situation will make her anxious and fearful of failure. Neither is it a particularly good offer for the woman who ranks security as an E. The newly created position may be phased out as other changes develop or as that particular project is completed. In any economy drive by the company it may fall victim to the job of 'last on, first off'.

17

Many of the characteristics that exist in newly created jobs also exist in new departments, with one exception. When an old, established department grows so large that it becomes unwieldy its duties may be divided into two departments. Because of their genesis, these two new groups have the long-term characteristics and potential of established groups.

A genuinely new department, or an open-ended and, especially, supervisory job may require workaholic tendencies. These jobs are for achievers who are willing to feel pushed, and willing to think about work after hours, in return for the wide opportunities inherent in the arrangement. Above all, these jobs are for people who can live with the knowledge that if the company's new project doesn't succeed, the whole department may be summarily disbanded.

QUESTION 4

What happened to the last occupants of your job?

Some of the answers and their interpretations are a replay of the 'How long has the supervisor had the job?' question. But it is an essential question for you no matter what your goals. It's *your* job we're discussing now. An answer of 'The last three people quit in less than a year' should give you pause. It may be the boss's personality, company politics, any number of things over which you will have no control. Better forget it.

Suppose the interviewer's answer to this and to other basic questions is 'I've only been here a few months. I don't know.' You can reply 'I'm looking forward to a long-term relationship with any company I join. Could you find out for me?' By *being prepared* in this way, you'll obtain the information you need.

QUESTION 5

Is the job you will be doing line or staff?

A line job is any job that contributes directly to the company's income. It *produces* the product or service the company sells. A staff position aids line with information, advice, services.

Because competence in line work is relatively easy to measure (Mary beat the quota this month!) your chances for being 'obviously successful' and consequently promotable are better in line positions than in staff positions. For the same reason, your chances for high income are better here also. But if success is conspicuous in line work, so is failure to meet a sales quota or a production schedule. Line means pressure, tension, constant challenge.

Because they are *not* on the direct producing/selling line, staff positions are usually less pressured. But they can be frustrating in a different way for the person who takes accomplishment and power seriously. In a staff job you may work for weeks or months on a customer research report, or on a new product design, or a new accounting system, or something similar. Then the line people *who make the final decision* may dismiss it, or delay it, or revise it.

Line holds final decision power because it does its own production/sales tasks directly. But staff as support supplies ideas and information *for other people's jobs*. In that situation the line person who receives the report or information is free to use it or leave it 'because if I accept your advice and it doesn't work out, I can't blame you. I'm the one who is responsible for the final decision.'

Some people in creative staff jobs become depressed when their advice is frequently passed over – 'I'm not getting any where. There's no satisfaction here.' Other people in staff thrive on the less pressured pace, the freedom from final responsibility.

QUESTION 6

What are the work conditions, hours, fringe benefits, in-company training, remuneration, etc.?

By now the interviewer should have mentioned most of these. Ask about those that matter to you but that you haven't yet heard about. For example, to you training courses may be an

E. Don't assume that a big company like this probably has a training programme. They may, but it may not cover your job or it may not be as complete as you expected. If training is important to you, ask for details of the company's policy. Well-run organisations usually have an employee manual explaining fringe benefits, which would include training, health insurance, sick pay, holidays, and so on. If a manual isn't available, get the specifics now.

If your interview with your supervisor was conducted away from your future workplace, ask the interviewer 'Could we walk through and see the area where I'll be working?' You're going to be living in that spot eight hours or more a day. Even a quick trip can allow you to check such workplace characteristics as noise, crowding, heat, privacy, loneliness or gregariousness, condition of work equipment, general area atmosphere. In moments like this it's interesting to observe how different goals affect different people's reactions and decisions. Perhaps they show you the tiny, partitioned office that goes with your new job. To you it looks lonely, unsociable, and unacceptable. Someone else may grab the job *just because* of that tiny, partitioned office. To her it may look like prestige and the beginning of power.

QUESTION 7

What kind of people run the company?

Traditional? Modern? A cohesive, homogeneous group? A varied, diversified group?

A company's attitude toward employees and customers is a reflection of the people who run the company. You'll find that traditional people run conservative organizations that tend to wait for something to happen in the industry and then react to it. Modern companies have managers who often anticipate the need for change and lead the way. In a tradition-dominated organisation you will have policies, rules, and methods for your job with little room for initiative and a strong aura of bureaucracy.

When the company – traditional or modern - is run by a

cohesive, homogeneous group, they will tend to judge your *capabilities* by your *external* characteristics. Fit their mould and they'll expect you to learn and blend in well. Appear 'different' and they'll be uncomfortable about trusting you with power, promotions, or even their friendship. If sociability on the job is important to you, a homogeneous group *where you fit the mould* can be ideal. You'll quickly become one of the gang. But if you don't match, you'll forever be an office outsider. A cohesive group means everyone in power is the same religion, and/or of the same ethnic extraction, and/or went to the same kind of college, and/or has the same intense political or leisure-time interests.

Anyone eager for promotion should avoid the cohesive group. Meeting their religious/ethnic criteria will not be enough. You are a woman and, for promotions, that makes you 'very different'. These people – especially when they are both cohesive and traditional – will have entrenched ideas about women's roles and women's jobs. The modern diversified company, as a result of its varied nature, will be much more likely to accept and promote women.

How do you obtain the necessary information about a company? If you're alert, some of the answers to questions 7 and 8 will emerge during your interview. Afterwards you can round out the picture. Ask among your friends until you locate someone who works for or knows that company. Talk to that person. And use your public library. It may have local newspaper articles about the company. If you live in a large metropolitan area, there may be an industrial directory of your city or county. Facts and figures in these volumes will give you many answers. There's also the directory of the local Chamber of Commerce, a free source of useful information about the character of member companies. Ask.

QUESTION 8

What is the company like? Expanding? Stable? Retrenching? What it means to you:

Expanding company
An expanding company is for you if you yearn for challenge,

opportunities to develop a variety of your talents, and promotion. In an expanding company the number of employees keeps growing. Because of the steady flow of new personnel and new activities, they regularly need new supervisors and executives. But this kind of work atmosphere is probably wrong for you if you long for peace, security, and an undemanding routine. In an expanding company you'll probably be subject to many upheavals, changes of organisation, and frequent demands for new kinds of work contributions.

Stable company
This kind of organisation probably offers you the greatest long-term security. An opening here is probably a job that has existed for years and will continue to exist. If it's a status title you're after and they offer it, you may be set for a lifetime career. In any job, competence means you can create a niche for yourself. New requirements in this environment are introduced gradually, allowing you time to adjust.

Not for the person in a hurry. Decisions are made with tested procedures. There is a 'company way'. Brilliant performance alone won't do it for you. They'll probably still expect you to queue up for reward.

Retrenching company
First you must find out what kind of retrenchment it is going through. Is the company in trouble generally? If so, it's obviously not a good choice. But perhaps it is just overexpanded and is cutting back to a healthy size. A job offer in the financially sound part of the company – that is, the division of the company that is showing a profit – could succeed very well.

CHAPTER 2.

How to recognise the best job: from now to 1990

It's this year, this month, and two capable, ambitious women start new jobs doing very similar work with two different companies. The first woman, Linda McPhillips, is employed by a consumer-credit reporting service. The second, Gail Staeger, is with a car manufacturing company. Five years later, Linda has been promoted two levels upwards in the company and has nearly tripled her initial salary. She has also had tempting offers from other consumer-credit organisations. Gail has had modest salary increases but is still plugging away at her original tasks. Gail has thought of changing jobs. She's tried, but she can find almost no openings with other industries where her experience would be valued.

Five years from now you can be woman 1 or woman 2! It doesn't matter whether you work in personnel, secretarial work, company finance, company publicity, or company management. What may often determine whether you are woman 1 or woman 2 is *the kind of business* your employer is engaged in.

Right now we already know which industries or kinds of businesses are likely to provide you with the widest and best job opportunities throughout the decade. You can use this knowledge to accept jobs in and concentrate your job hunting among the 'seven best'. They are:

Accounting
At professional level in accounting, private industry and civil service.

Computing
Programmers, systems analysts, etc.

Craft apprenticeships
Carpentry, masonry, engineering, electricians.

Engineering
In all fields and at all levels.

Science and engineering technology
All phases of production and marketing.

Law enforcement

Sales
Securities, cars, estate agencies, insurance, industrial, wholesale to retail.

When people first hear the names of the fastest-growing industries, they frequently don't realise they *already* have the skills to succeed in these occupations.

People say 'Oh, I don't know anything about computers or business services.' Or 'I'm no good at maths so I can't go into finance.' They overlook the fact that these industries need secretaries, managers, clerks, sales people, personnel people, public relations people, top executives – as well as technical specialists who actually work with the computers.

But then many still are puzzled. They ask 'So if you're going to be a clerk or bookkeeper, or executive or administrator or secretary or whatever, what difference does it make if you work for one of the fastest growing industries or for other kinds of industries?'

Could be a big difference. An 'ordinary' job with one of the best industries can be much better. First, because the industry is growing, companies keep hiring. Anyone who is competent has no worries about layoffs. Next, since the

24

industry is growing, there are continual new opportunities for supervisory jobs as new employees are hired and new departments are formed. If you join one of these growing companies, you're there on the scene. You're acquiring expertise in that business. You may start at a low level – as a clerk – but when a better job opens up (which happens constantly in the expanding business), you often can apply for it and get it. Even if the better job is in another department and requires much more responsibility from you, the boss is under pressure to fill the position quickly. The boss is acquainted with you, knows you understand many of the details of that business. The average boss is often glad to promote you because it saves him or her the exhausting (and time-consuming) task of interviewing applicants and then breaking in the new employee.

However, things can be different if you work in a declining industry. You might be a super secretary or sales person or manager. If the industry is having problems, companies have to cut back and you might be laid off despite your good record. Even if you keep your position, how many promotion openings can you look forward to in a sick industry? Opportunities will be contracting, not expanding. You won't even have much chance for routine pay increases. The boss will say 'Business is bad. We can't afford it.'

That is exactly what happened with Linda McPhillips and Gail Staeger. Because consumer-credit service is part of one of the fastest-growing industries Linda has had a rapid rise in her job title and salary. Because Gail is working in an industry which is not expanding, she has had a very different experience. She has found it impossible to move upwards within her company or out to a better job elsewhere. The truth is that Gail is fortunate to still have her job. Many of her co-workers who were just as competent were made redundant simply because the shrinking business needed fewer employees.

CHAPTER **3.**

Career quiz: are your job ideas ready for the 1980s?

The dazzling career opportunities available to women in the 1980s will be useless to you if your job attitudes prevent you from accepting what could be yours.

If often shocks people – women as well as men – to discover that though they believe they support careers for women, *some* of their ideas reflect the nineteenth century rather than the late twentieth century. It's the result, of course, of the mental compartmentalisation that plagues us all. If we have occasion to think about a topic, we examine it and update our views. But *portions* of the subject go unexamined and without our realising it we retain attitudes and pockets of ideas we might reject if we had the necessary facts and gave the matter some thought.

To discover if you have brought your views into the 1980s, try the true-false quiz here – together with the research facts that support the modern, career facts for women.

1. Women who go into men-only luncheon and social clubs and try to break down the men-only rules are wasting effort on an unimportant kind of discrimination.

2. Some business districts are deserted at night and it's understandable if women aren't offered executive jobs in

that area. Executives often have to put in overtime and a woman supervisor might find herself in an unsafe situation.

3. If you are promoted and have men assigned to work for you, they will probably readily accept you as the boss.

4. Women in general aren't any more emotional on the job than men are.

5. If the job involves a lot of travel, a company shouldn't offer it to a woman with children.

6. Educated, ambitious women are socially unattractive to men.

7. It's very important, when appropriate, to use words like *businessperson, chairperson,* and *people-made* instead of *businessman, chairman,* and *man-made.*

8. You can't change a man's negative attitudes towards careers for women.

9. Though women have many human relations business talents, they are not really comfortable thinking about money or dealing with fiscal realities.

10. Women in general are very good at creating new ideas and being leaders.

Answers

1. *False.* It really is very important to your job chances that men-only luncheon and social clubs be abolished.

Expense-account business meals have become a central part of business life because so much business is transacted at these tables. If a club will not admit women, it amounts to denying the women the business opportunities, business contacts, discussions, and information they could have acquired there. In addition, because employers know a woman will be unable to represent the company adequately at business meetings in these clubs, they frequently hesitate to offer a woman the job. If a woman does get the job, by being excluded she is unfairly hampered in succeeding at her job.

2. *False.* Women should certainly be offered the positions.

When women work at such non-executive jobs as telephone operators, nurses, night-shift factory assemblers, charwomen, baby sitters, and the like nobody thinks of denying them the positions because of night dangers. They're expected to be adults who can arrange to get safely to and from work. Why then, when a woman is about to get a high-level job, should it be assumed she lacks the intelligence to arrange for safe night transportation?

3. *True.* Right this minute millions of men are taking orders from hundreds of thousands of women bosses.

While the media continue to produce anxious discussions about 'Will men work for women?', the question is already answered. Millions of men already do work for women bosses. And month by month more and more men are acquiring women managers. *Just as they would with any boss, the men try to keep their own jobs by working well for their female supervisors.* There are women in charge of blue-collar factory and craft workers of all kinds and in charge of offices, shops, banks, company departments, and corporate activities of every conceivable type. In your own organisation right now aren't women supervising men as well as women? Britain has had women Cabinet Ministers since before the War – and a woman Prime Minister famous for her toughness.

The success of all new bosses, male as well as female, depends on their acceptance by subordinates. Hundreds of thousands of women bosses are succeeding. Why shouldn't you?

4. *True.* Women in general are no more emotional on the job than men are.

Scientific studies have repeatedly indicated that women are better able to cope with stress than are men. Scientists believe this is one of the major reasons women as a group live longer than men do. As for behaviour in crises, as one analyst put it: 'Women are not considered too emotional to cope with the life-and-death situations in a hospital or in the home but somehow there is the fear that a profit-and-loss crisis will shatter them.'

5. *False.* They should be allowed to decide whether they want the travel jobs.

Many married men are unwilling to accept positions requiring travel. But no one considers 'protecting' all men from such job offers. Individual men are seen as adults capable of controlling their own lives who should consider and decide job offers for themselves. Women should receive the same treatment. They too are adults. You might not be interested in such a job. Fine. Make your own career decisions and support the right of other women to make theirs.

6. *False.* Styles in women who are attractive to men change from decade to decade.

Victorian women had to faint and flutter to be considered feminine and attractive to men. (Remember in *Little Women* how unacceptable Jo is because she refuses to do so.) Today's man would regard a woman who swooned as a kook to be avoided. During the 1930s, 1940s, and 1950s, in order to be attractive, women had to act helpless, dumb, and indecisive – the clinging vine was a popular type. How many men do you know nowadays who want to be stuck with a woman who has to be guided and propped up all through life because she's 'helpless'?

And the style continues to change. As men learn first to enjoy and then to depend on the psychological security and the material comforts of a two-pay-cheque family, their attitudes toward women's careers are altering noticeably. It is almost impossible now to go to a party and not discover men who clearly feel their wives' burgeoning careers reflect credit on the husband and the family.

Just as the behaviour of the 1920s woman made the swooning, fluttering Victorian female obsolete and the 1960s women made the 1920s-to-1950s 'dumb' clinging vine uninteresting, so men's experiences with the new exciting, ambitious woman will transform men's expectations of what is an attractive woman.

7. *True.* It's important to use words like *businesspeople, chairperson, people-made.*

Even though it might sound strange or even awkward at

first, as all new words do, there is too much at stake to worry about a relatively unimportant consideration like an unfamiliar sound. Words define, reinforce, *and to a large extent control the way people see and run their lives.* As long as general discussions of work are always done in terms of businessmen, manhours, the right man for the job, and chairman, *we are strengthening the average person's picture of the job world as being 'naturally' male with women as interlopers.*

When we change our language to *include* both sexes, we change the mental image people have of who naturally belongs in the work world. By altering our vocabulary we create a sex-free business environment where it now seems natural for women to be considered for well-paying, higher-level jobs.

8. *False.* During the last few decades men have changed many of their basic ideas about women's careers.

For example, in the 1930s it was thought that it was the husband's duty to support his wife. Most men would have been embarrassed to have working wives. Only 10 per cent of married women *did* work, which made them very unusual. And even those women usually stopped working once they started a family. Today people's attitudes are not only changed, they are completely opposite! If a young married woman left her job before she had children, people would wonder why she was acting so strangely.

After World War II men's attitudes towards women and careers continued to change. Married women without children worked with universal approval. Gradually, women with children began to go back to work, too. Today, around 30 per cent of women with a child under five are working (most work part-time). And when it comes to women with children under the age of ten, almost three-quarters are working. Again, the majority of them work part-time. Almost all the growth in employment in Britain in the 1970s was due to the increased numbers of women coming back into the labour force for part-time work. Their numbers increased by a million women.

As late as the 1970s men generally believed the only

reasons women worked are 'to get out of the house' or 'for pin money'. In fact, about one in six households relies on a woman for financial support. (There are three-quarters of a million single-parent families headed by women, for a start.) With inflation and rising costs, it is now recognised that most households need two incomes to raise them above the poverty line.

The average man has become aware that the woman working at the desk next to him is not there to amuse herself. She is there for the same reasons men are. Many of the remaining masculine misconceptions about women and careers can disappear in the 1980s.

9. *False. Within the privacy of their families* women have long been recognised as being very competent with money.

The way couples deal with their money varies around the country and from family to family, but most studies have found that the wives are usually responsible for day-to-day household expenses. Whether they get an unopened pay-packet from their husbands, or a flat housekeeping allowance, or variable handouts, it is the women's job to manage that money and budget for food and other necessities. Often that includes paying all routine bills. The majority of families, today and in the past, have relied on the women to understand and successfully deal with the family's fiscal realities.

Sylvia Auerbach, author of *A Woman's Book of Money* (Doubleday) and *The Women's Guide to Managing Money* (O Publications), is an expert on personal financial matters who has lectured, headed seminars, and organised and chaired university courses on financial management. She has observed that women in our society are taught to suppress their natural competence with money. 'Over and over,' Ms Auerbach says, 'I notice that many women believe it is "unfeminine" to admit to fiscal skill. If they do handle the family money, they think it reflects poorly on the male in their life if anyone finds out. Because of these social pressures, other women who certainly have the intelligence and natural ability to deal logically with financial matters accept the stereotype that they "can't" and don't even try.'

As times are changing and women are moving into management-executive positions, their natural talent with money is surfacing – many are concentrating on occupations that demand fiscal-mathematical skill. The percentage of graduates who are women going into banking, insurance and finance increased from 22 to 31 per cent between 1971 and 1981. Over the same period, the percentage of graduates who were women going into accountancy increased even more – from 8 to nearly 28 per cent.

10. *True.* In general women seem to be *more* talented than men when it comes to creating ideas and equally capable of leadership.

Until recently the problem has been that though women are born with the abilities, they have been taught not to use them.

The Johnson O'Connor Research Foundation, an American nationwide research organisation, has tested more than half a million men and women for work aptitudes during the past half century. Their research reveals that more women than men are high in the kinds of creative thinking and general mental ability required to succeed as bankers, managers executives, politicians, chemists, lawyers, physicians, insurance adjusters, teachers, writers, sales representatives, and the like. Altogether the foundation has isolated and tested for twenty-one aptitudes. One of the abilities they call *ideaphoria*, a measure of the rate of flow of ideas. In any group of 1,000 women and 1,000 men, they report that more women than men will be talented in ideaphoria. Based on inborn aptitudes alone, concludes the foundation, there ought to be more female executives than male.

Other experts have noted women's natural leadership ability. Dr Arthur A. Witkin, chief psychologist for Personnel Sciences Center in New York City, which has helped employers select 50,000 employees for hiring or promotion since 1948, has observed that 'There is only one personality factor that separates executive and entrepreneur women from their male counterparts – and in this factor women are generally superior.'

Dr Witkin explains that contrary to the myths this superior feminine quality is 'independence which includes the ability to make a decision without a committee to support it and also emotional detachment that allows the person to see herself-himself and surroundings objectively, as well as an ability to react to criticism without undue sensitivity.' On the average, he continues, 'women rank higher in these areas than males *who are on their employment level*, based on our psychological test results, evaluations during personal interviews, and the experience of employees who come to us for career counselling.' [Emphasis added.]

As more and more women realise that leadership is 'feminine' and is as flattering to women as to men, more women will permit themselves to use their natural talents.

33

PART **II**

MAKING THEM REALISE
YOU'RE 'GOOD'

CHAPTER 4.

Twelve ways to make the right impression

If you handle yourself right, you can avoid many job problems. Doing it right and making the right impression causes others to see you as both competent and pleasant. People with that reputation escape many daily hassles. No one's worklife is completely trouble-free. But, overall, the people who make the right impression find that co-workers tend to cooperate with them and that their bosses notice and reward good performance.

Don't set up unrealistic impressions

Your boss asks 'Do you think you can do this by five-thirty tomorrow?' You quickly look the assignment over and since you're anxious to impress with your efficiency you reply 'I can probably have it finished before lunch tomorrow.'

You're an excellent worker, but this project really does require almost two days' effort. With interruptions and attending to your other non-deferrable duties, it takes you till past five-thirty the next day. Your boss has left for home and you present it the morning after with explanations and apologies for its being late.

By setting up unrealistic expectations you've undercut

your own image. Instead of appearing to be the bright, efficient person you are, you've made yourself look slow and even undependable. After all, you were the one who volunteered to get it done before lunch. For any assignment – a sales goal, schedule, production goal, whatever – a conservative estimate is always best. It's a sure-win policy. If it takes as long as your conservative projection, then you look knowledgeable and competent. If you outdo your careful estimate and complete it earlier, you make yourself look like a whizkid and a treasure.

Speak no evil

When discussing past jobs you've held and other co-workers and bosses, be discreet. Passing on bits of negative gossip and witty criticism will cause others to back off. At the moment they may enjoy your comments, but they will view you as lacking good business sense. And they will fear that someday at another job you will be attacking those you are now working with.

Promptness

After you volunteer to come in on one of your days off you realise that arriving on time will be a problem. Will your boss understand when you are late? Probably not. Even if you agreed to come in as a favour to your supervisor, business behaviour demands that once you accept the assignment, you must be prompt.

Drink

Your employer has no objections to employees having a drink or even two at lunch when people eat out. Yet you've heard there is a company rule against anyone keeping alcohol on company premises.

You often give your boss extra effort by skipping lunch and working and eating at your desk. In the circumstances would it be wrong to keep a small supply of alcohol and add it to a lunchtime can of ginger ale?

You'd be courting trouble. Companies make a definite distinction between drinking off and on the premises. And the courts and arbitrators have a long history of supporting the employer and disciplining employees for possession of alcohol at work *if* the company rule is well known to employees and consistently enforced.

Find out, don't guess

Boardroom Reports, a major management newsletter, points out that one of the most common causes of unsatisfactory job performance is employee timidity about asking questions. Because they fail to clear up ambiguities or to obtain all the facts they need, people misunderstand some of their job responsibilities. Naturally, if you don't understand what's expected of you, you can't perform well enough to please your superiors.

Putting yourself down

You've noticed that at other jobs you've held your boss and co-workers seldom seemed to give you credit for your good ideas and suggestions. In fact, others sometimes later expressed the same views you had already offered and received a positive response and 'credit'.

You may be sabotaging yourself by the way you present your ideas. Perhaps in your attempts to offer your comments without sounding pushy or arrogant you've fallen into the habit of beginning with something like 'This may sound like a silly idea' or 'I'm probably not absolutely right about this' or 'This may not be worth much but . . .' By prefacing your ideas in this way, you suggest they aren't worthwhile. You produce an attitude of disinterest in others. And why not? You yourself warned them that what you were going to say was silly or wrong or not worth much.

Every job is different

The same job title doesn't mean the same job content. At any new job expect to have to learn your duties and how this particular employer wants them performed. One assistant to a vice-president discovered her responsibilities included interviewing applicants for certain clerical jobs. Previously, with the same title, Assistant to the Vice-President, she had had nothing to do with job applicants. Some of the extras you're handed may broaden your credentials and may later provide your best opportunities to quality for pay increases and better jobs. If there are some tasks – such as serving coffee – you don't want to accept, mention them during the *final* negotiations (after you have your job offer) and before you start work.

Staying late

You have a dinner date and now your boss suddenly asks you to stay after hours and help catch up on the workload. He cannot make you do things you are not contracted to do, and your contract with the firm may make it clear whether or not you are expected to work extra hours and get paid for them.

Obviously, if there is something really urgent to be done you will not improve your standing with the boss – or the organisation – by putting your date first. But if you are often asked to do overtime, especially at short notice, it is either because your department is under-staffed or you are inefficient. In the first case, discuss the problem with your supervisor; in the second, look carefully at your own routines and where you may be losing time.

The Factories Act and some other Acts set maximum working hours for women factory workers, and restrict their employment on shifts or nightwork, and limit overtime work. Details of these provisions, and of other aspects of working women's rights, are given in a useful book by Tess Gill and Larry Whitty: *Women's Rights in the Workplace* (Pelican).

Getting help from co-workers

Your response to others' requests will determine whether you receive help when you need it. No one expects you to neglect your own goals. But an attitude of cooperation is essential. Everyone has met someone like Mary Petares. Mary's attitude is 'Why should I let other people pick my brains?' When others ask how Mary solved some past job problem, she usually replies 'Oh, I really don't remember.' She is equally standoffish about anyone 'butting into my territory'. At coffee break or lunch if someone tries to discuss a new idea that eases the work or solves a problem, Mary makes it clear she doesn't need any advice. It never seems to occur to Mary that she can listen pleasantly and then ignore the idea if it doesn't seem useful.

Those who work with Mary quickly learn neither to ask for help nor to offer it. All of this leaves Mary in a dangerous situation. On the days when she is the one who needs help, advice, or information, she's upset and troubled because people are so uncooperative.

Personal habits

One woman remembers being told by an annoyed co-worker, 'You're forever borrowing something.' The co-worker tried to make it sound like a teasing remark, yet the critical content was clear. Another woman was sometimes chided by her previous boss for 'never being at your desk when I need you'. Be honest with yourself. What have your co-workers or bosses complained of or joked about? Did they consider you careless about deadlines? Abrupt with subordinates? Too quick to lose your temper? Whatever your irritating personal habits, devote special effort to improving that part of your job performance. If those actions alienated co-workers in the past, they will almost certainly make the wrong impression and irritate your present colleagues.

He calls you 'honey'

Though it's not done in a sexually harassing manner, you feel it is a subtle putdown of you as a competent worker every time your boss or a co-worker addresses you as 'honey', 'dear', or a similar term. How can you persuade them to stop without turning the situation into a confrontation?

You're right to feel annoyed, but even a simply reply of 'Please don't call me that' will probably produce hostility *towards you.* (Illogical, but that's human nature.) Instead, a quiet response such as 'I really like being called Nancy' or 'My good friends call me Nancy' ought soon to have an effect on all but the most obtuse.

Male co-workers who put an arm around you or in some friendly, non-sexual manner 'commend' you with their hands also should not be tolerated. Industrial psychologists have discovered that this kind of body language is subconsciously interpreted by others as indicating you are the subordinate in the relationship and under his direction. When you're a member of the team and his equal (or superior) that's definitely not the impression you want others to have.

The five essentials

Elton Reeves, management consultant and author of *How to Get Along with Almost Everybody* (Amacom), offers five basic ways to make a good impression and then maintain good permanent relationships: (1) Be positive and optimistic. Human nature usually reacts to you on the same emotional level it is approached on. (2) Go a little out of your way to demonstrate your positive attitude. (3) Don't be an information bottleneck. Pass on all information others need. Reeves says this does more to tear down or build your reputation with others than anything else. (4) Be intellectually honest. This means you do not deliberately 'misunderstand' orders or work conditions. It also requires that you avoid gossip that delicately twists what others say or do. (5) Don't expect too much active friendship. Overall, this is a work relationship, all that is necessary is that you move pleasantly through the day together. Reeves sums it up. 'You will be most successful if you take the attitude that the greatest responsibility for your acceptance or rejection by others rests on your shoulders.'

CHAPTER **5.**

How to look good at a meeting

Looking good at meetings is probably the quickest and simplest way to impress the people who can affect your job future. There they are, all of them: your boss, your peers, maybe your boss's boss. No telephone interruptions, no desk-clutter distractions, everyone paying attention. Except for your immediate superior, others usually have only a hazy idea of the work you do and how well you do it. But if you perform well at meetings, you create for yourself an *overall* positive image that everybody notices. They're left with the clear impression that you're good, you're a winner.

Conversely, of course, fumbling and foot-in-mouth at meetings can be disastrous. You leave with the impression that you 'just don't have what it takes'.

Whatever you can learn about looking good at meetings will help you balance the built-in uneven odds against you. Business get-togethers are probably the only team situation where participants are unequally matched. Members of athletic sports teams are approximately equal in experience, age, and skill. Throughout your school years, those you competed against scholastically were no further along than you in life experience. But now at your business meetings some of the people may be literally twice as old as you.

They've been attending meetings for as long as you've been alive. And *some* of them have learned a good deal about making themselves look good – at times, at the expense of others. Others, though still young, have already picked up a lot. Fortunately for you, many other people have learned very little. They may have been sitting at meetings for years, even decades, yet they've never bothered to analyse what was happening around them. By using the following information, you can go a long way towards making your meeting perform-ance the equal of anyone's.

There are three basic ways you can make yourself look good at a meeting by (1) Your own positive actions; (2) avoiding damaging actions; that is, by seeing to it that you don't do yourself in; and (3) blocking others' attempts to make you look bad.

Since 'constructive and effective' are the key characteris-tics you're trying to project, *positive* thought and behaviour should be your basic strategy. Even when you feel a proposed idea must be eliminated, never come out against it. Instead, always be *for* another approach.

This is necessary because we're dealing with that volatile force called your image. Even if your attack on an idea is sensible and well phrased, you are nevertheless left appearing an obstructionist. By being *for* another approach you achieve the same results and are seen as someone 'with great constructive ability'.

Above all, keep in mind that everyone sitting there prob-ably feels as vulnerable as you do. Even mild criticism of others' performance will make you instant enemies. 'She knifed me in public' is the way they'll tell it later. If you do offer a better idea, save the other person's ego with some-thing like 'That's a good idea; could we also look at it from this angle?' Never be lured into doing a hatchet job on some-one or something. In addition to the enemies you will make, your allies will also mark you as dangerous.

Always pause before you attempt to deflect a bad idea and ask yourself 'Why am I the one doing this?' Yes, it's true everybody should have the interest of the department and company at heart. But if you're going to appoint yourself ombudswoman and fight everyone's battles for them, you can be sure they're going to let you. When the proposal affects others directly and you only peripherally, let it be. If they're not willing to speak up for themselves, why should you do it? If you use up your skills on their battles, you may not be able to win your own. When you do struggle for something worthwhile, recognise the moment to stop. As soon as the boss says 'Okay, this is what we'll do,' stop. Discussion time is over. Every contrary word you utter now will count hard against you.

Knowing beforehand that you're going to be in the spotlight delivering a report or presentation is a silver-platter opportunity to look good. Think out your remarks. Make a list of points you'll want to cover. Practise running through them aloud until you can state them clearly in an appropriate time segment – but not a memorised speech or a written speech. Both are deadly. Remember, too, you're facing a TV-trained audience. Anything you can create – charts, mimeographed handouts, blackboard diagrams – that people can watch as you talk will help you rivet your colleagues' attention. 'She's good' will be everyone's final mental verdict.

After you prepare and believe you'll do well, see if you can arrange to have an influential superior sit in. Any superior concerned with the topic is a logical person to invite. The more upper-echelon people you can corral to see you on your big days, the better.

Now that you are prepared, avoid falling into the common feminine error of blowing it with your first few minutes of off-the-cuff behaviour. In these transition times, as women move into positions of authority in business, many are torn by their own inner double self-image. Though they're competent at their jobs, many women feel it obligatory to do a few minutes of girlish fluttering before launching into a businesslike presentation. These few minutes of giggle-and-gush are thrown off as a kind of propitiatory offering to the bigots in the room. 'See, competent women aren't really threatening bitches. Look how "feminine" I am' is the clear unspoken message during these episodes.

It doesn't work. The bigots remain unconvinced while with

everyone else your standing as a level-headed woman is severely damaged. Even a super presentation will not completely undo the opening foolishness.

Having no predetermined role at a meeting does not free you from the need to prepare. Betty Lehan Harragan, author of *Games Mother Never Taught You* (Warner); warns that 'Before every routine meeting men make it their business to find out what the topics will be. If a man has an idea he wants approved, he circulates and lines up a few allies beforehand, he tries to sound out opposing viewpoints and mentally prepares counter ideas. Women tend to go in and try to succeed while shooting from the hip with no foreknowledge of what's going to be discussed, who's for it, who's against. It's not the way to look good.

'Intelligent choice of your seat can also aid your image. Don't bury yourself inconspicuously. If seating is unstructured, put yourself with the powerful people. Everyone else will wonder whether you're one of the new favourites and their thoughts will aid you.'

Sometimes how you look at a meeting passes from your initiative to the actions of others. When there is something important that you expect to have discussed, be alert for those who would shove you into the background. The person or prearranged team that announces 'Let's resolve the XYZ problem' and then starts discussing it is attempting to sandbag everyone into following their private agenda.

Speak out. 'Bill, we can add the XYZ problem to the agenda if we have time. The ABC topic is *already* on the agenda.' Then, if you can, launch into it. Infighting among others is another potential danger to you. Group members may seem to be talking about the meeting's topics but they may really be concentrating on displaying themselves or putting someone else down. Recognize these performances. Then save your breath and your image. No one will evaluate your conciliatory suggestions honestly and you may get mauled in the crossfire.

Idea thieves who operate at meetings are a special kind of problem advertising expert Jane Trahey has given considerable thought to. In *Jane Trahey on Women and Power* (Rawson

Associates) she suggests that you respond fast when you hear words such as 'That's a nice idea. I'll work on it and put it into shape.' The speaker is about to turn *your* idea into 'my idea'. 'How do you spell that again?' He or she is taking notes on your words, and unless you clearly lay claim now the idea will soon be presented to the boss as someone else's brainchild. Says Ms Trahey, when everyone is told to bring ideas to a meeting, women bring ideas and men will come back with sharp pencils. If you possibly can, she adds, avoid giving out your good ideas at meetings. They are in constant danger of becoming public property. Offer them in written form, making clear the ideas are yours.

Eventually the day may come when someone openly attacks you at a meeting. If you've done your routine preparation, your antennae ought to have picked up intimations of trouble. Still, even the best-organised people can be ambushed. When that happens, cling steadfastly to your positive attitude. It becomes both your defence and your offence. Martin Smith, author of *I Hate to See a Manager Cry* (Addison-Wesley), has refined the positive response to attack to two-step perfection. First, keep your voice level. Don't get excited. Emotion will make people think there may be something to the comments. (Sure, it's hard to do – but think how great you'll feel and look when you win.) Second, don't say 'You're wrong.' Put it positively: 'I see what you mean, but there are some facts that you may not be aware of. Once you have a chance after the meeting to study the whole picture you may change your mind.'

Now you've put your opponents on the defensive. You've made it seem they are irresponsible, that they spoke without checking every aspect. Since you said it would take time 'after the meeting' to study the situation, they can't force your hand here. Just stick to your response, broken-record style if necessary. The more they persist, the more *they* now look emotional and dangerously uninterested in the truth.

In short, once again you'll end up looking good at a meeting.

CHAPTER **6.**

How to win
the memo game

You really don't have a choice about whether or not you'll play the 'memo game'. In most organisations it is an everyday part of office politics. Even the person who refuses to 'get involved' finds herself used by co-workers as part of *their* politicking. Since being the passive victim in other people's games can't possibly help your career, you must protect yourself by understanding the plays others are making and by taking part.

Of course, you should use memos for their basic function of passing along information. You can also use memos to (1) help you get ahead on your job; (2) protect yourself from job hassles and disasters; (3) interpret bosses' and co-workers' plans and goals.

Tell your boss how you're doing

When you're instructed to drop one assignment for another, begin a new project, change a procedure, or do anything that is a change in your work routine, it may take time before the results of your efforts become visible. A short memo indicating how you've begun, followed by progress reports to your boss, will indicate you are following through. It will comfort your boss. You can be relied upon and do not need prodding or close supervision. Bosses like such people.

Don't hide your light, etc.

The payoff for hard work alone is not very much. Results are worth more. Don't assume your boss knows you are a doer just because you are always busy. You have to point out some of your accomplishments.

You can't blow your own trumpet. But you can report to your boss and others involved with memos on tasks completed and on situations. For example, 'Don't worry about the Derby project. Though three people in my department are out with the flu [or on vacation or whatever], I'll have it completed on time. I'm using two temporaries and staying overtime.'

The *Wall Street Journal* recently reported that a survey had revealed 83 per cent of top executives who were fired shared a common trait: they had failed to point out their work achievements to their superiors at the proper time. They mistakenly depended on 'good work speaking for itself'. If top executives who have built-in visibility in an organisation must strive to have their achievements noticed, it is even more true for people in lesser positions.

The unusual can be important

Have you ever received a letter of commendation from a customer or client? Did they tell you on the phone how much they appreciated your efforts? Have you received any recognition of the job in some way work- or company-related? Don't bury it! Modesty can be expensive. Send a photocopy of any document you received with a 'For your information' memo to your boss. Or straightforwardly report the event if there is nothing to photocopy. In either case ask that a copy of the memo and any related documents be inserted in your personnel file. That's where they look during merit review and promotion time.

Follow-up – one memo may beget another

You will receive memos. If one requires a response, refer to the memo topic and date at the beginning of your reply. It provides continuity. If you want any follow-through to your memo, be specific. You use your final sentence to produce your response, such as 'Please let me know by Monday the 22nd if you want a product-packaging meeting scheduled for Wednesday the 24th.'

When you have to remind a superior who didn't follow through, try a little subtlety. Find a sensible reason for the second memo, such as additional details about the plan the executive might want to consider. This gives you the opportunity to restate your original request. It is easy to be carried away in replying to memos that are replies to memos that are replies, on and on. Stop before you look either silly or neurotic.

Carbon copies can protect you

Using memos to protect yourself requires judgment and a sense of timing. You must appraise each situation critically. Flooding people with memos lessens the impact of what you write. They may begin treating your important ones as casually as those which are not so important. But neither should you become the scapegoat, because you have nothing on paper.

For example, you may receive verbal instructions or approval for some assignment that involves spending money. You follow through. When the invoice arrives from the supplier, you are asked why the purchase was made. It seems that the company began a cost reduction programme *after* you received the approval from your boss. Any verbal 'he said', 'she said' can be easily disputed by your boss, who can claim you misunderstood the instructions. A carbon of the memo you sent your boss acknowledging the verbal authorisation can save you embarrassment and recrimination.

Carbons are also a protective device in dealing with co-workers. You have a deadline to meet, but you can't complete your assignment until you receive some data from another employee. At today's meeting a co-worker agreed to give you the information by a certain date. You can follow up with a memo to the other person mentioning the information you're to be given and the agreed-on due date. A carbon to your boss and to others involved in the project – plus your file copy – could keep you from becoming the scapegoat if you can't meet your deadline because your co-worker misses hers. Other times carbon copies (cc:) to your boss and to others involved in a project can provide the stimulus that will prompt your co-worker to deliver on time. You head these memos 'Situation Statement'.

Carbons also keep everyone a little more honourable. They can prevent your ideas from being stolen. When you send a memo outlining an original idea or proposal to everyone who might be affected, you make sure no one else will claim authorship of your idea.

Memos flow like the river: which do you read?

You learn to understand your co-workers and your superiors better if you watch for patterns in their memos. The types of subjects they concentrate on reveal their anxieties and their goals.

By comprehending the reasons behind the piles of memos you can also simplify your own life. Some memos will continue to require your close attention. Others will require only a glance because you will realise they were sent for political purposes and not to transmit information you need. Incidentally, it is these hidden human reasons for churning out memos that defeat all the efficiency-drive approaches to limiting their production.

Memos pile into your in-tray for the same reasons you are sending yours. They come from people who want to protect themselves, to make themselves visible, and to make themselves look efficient. In addition, most organisations have a few employees who find it easier to turn out memos about work projects than to tackle the projects themselves. Others use memos as a means of inflating their egos and announcing 'I'm in charge of this project.' Still others are foolishly indiscriminate about their 'cc' list and send everything to everybody.

Memos are a mirror

What and how you write is a reflection of yourself. Do your memos show you are organised and competent? Are they neat and correctly written? Every company or every boss has a preferred format for memos. Use that format. It will look familiar and make it easier to read and be more likely to bring you a prompt response.

The subject heading should be specific and complete. 'Sales Meeting Plan' is not enough'; 'Plan for February Sales Meeting' is. If you can't write the memo topic in a succinct phrase or short sentence, you haven't organised your thoughts adequately. Before writing a memo, rough-draft what you want to convey. After all, even Jane Austen rewrote.

List the important points and write as briefly as possible. Long memos are frequently skimmed and misinterpreted. Highlight any solutions, recommendations, or conclusions. If a sequence is involved, number: 1, 2, 3. It directs the reader's attention and makes for clarity.

Write always with your recipient in mind. You want your message understood and acted upon.

Don't manufacture unnecessary enemies for yourself

Never write a memo in anger. You're sure to say something you'll later regret. If you are in a supervisory position and have to issue a written warning to a subordinate, don't send copies to anyone else. Keep the carbon in your private files. If you have to consult a colleague on a sensitive company issue, do so orally rather than by putting your current views into a memo. And never be conned into writing potentially embarrassing memos by some adept, smooth-talking co-worker or supervisor. If your opponents eventually triumph, you're not going to want permanent evidence in people's files of your having campaigned for the loser.

Remember that even confidential memos are sometimes

read by the wrong people. If you know it would be disastrous for you if Ms X or Mr Y happened to see or hear of this memo, why write it? Trust your instincts. Whenever you have the uneasy feeling that what you're writing may someday come back to haunt you, tear it up and find a less permanent way to disseminate your views and information.

CHAPTER 7.

How to read – and react to – other people's body language

You may have read books and articles explaining body language, but have you ever realised that *responding* to body language can help you succeed at your job?

You, like everyone else, have probably been talking in body language gestures and subconsciously reading them all your life. When you meet someone, spend fifteen minutes in casual conversation, and then say to yourself 'What a phoney!', your subconscious has probably noticed that the body language didn't match the spoken words. When your bosses or co-workers assure you they'll support your request yet you somehow feel you shouldn't trust their promises, you've probably read the body language.

As we grow up, we all learn to control what comes out of our mouths. We learn tact and discretion – when to keep silent and when to agree. Our tongues learn, but our bodies never do. Body language experts believe that only a pathological liar or a superb actor can fake what the body says.

As a result, every working day we are surrounded by people whose gestures are delivering messages. Depending on your subconscious to interpret the constant flow of body statement is too slow. You can *respond* better when you bring the reading to a conscious level, when you learn to recognise

53

the signals immediately. Then if the message reads 'I'm not convinced', you can pause. Depending on the circumstances, you might ask 'Do you want me to explain this more thoroughly?' or 'Does some of this seem impractical?'

'Well, as a matter of fact . . .' the other person says.

Once the problem is explained, you can often supply the desired answer. Then the other person may say 'Yes, I see.'

By recognising the body language, you've turned the situation from 'I'm not convinced' resistance to cooperation.

Gerard I. Nierenberg, a lawyer who specialises in business and government negotiating, and Henry H. Calero, a negotiation consultant and business executive, have concentrated on body language in the business world. They have videotaped 2,500 business negotiation sessions and obtained participant feedback from those involved. From their research they've noted a variety of 'gesture clusters' people unconsciously use to express open-ness, defensiveness, thoughtfulness, suspicion, readiness, reassurance, cooperation, frustration, confidence, nervousness, self-control, boredom, expectancy, superiority, and so on (*How to Read a Person Like a Book*, Simon & Schuster). Like all body language experts, Nierenberg and Calero have profited from the scientific stature given the subject by Dr Ray Birdwhistell, the University of Pennsylvania professor of communication who moved it from a vague 'art' to a science that can be analysed and systematised.

Dr Birdwhistell and every body language specialist caution that isolated gestures are meaningless. You must interpret gestures within the setting and circumstances and as a part of a combination of body movement, facial expressions, and voice tone.

Within that understanding, Nierenberg and Calero believe the following are some of the significant 'gesture clusters'. We've added suggestions of *what to do about* the body statements.

Defensiveness

When you see a cluster of gestures like arms folded high on chest, hands locked in front or behind in fists, hands gripping the chair arms, locked ankles, leaning away from you, turning the body sideways away from you, it's definitely time to think back and try to understand what has just been said or done that caused the problem. Change your direction, pause, try new approaches to dissolve the tension.

Readiness

Hands on hips or hands on mid-thigh when seated, sitting or leaning forward on the edge of chair, moving closer to you – all indicate others are convinced and now will be impatient if you indulge in further preliminaries. 'Let's get on with it' is what their bodies are saying.

Thoughtfulness, evaluating

Chin-stroking, chewing on spectacles or spectacle-wiping, or slow ritualistic lighting of pipe are attempts to gain time to think. Don't rush the other person.

Someone sitting toward the edge of the chair, body leaning forward, head slightly tilted, supported by one hand, is very interested. If you need someone at this point to agree that the project is worth investigating, here's your person.

However, there's a slightly different pose that usually indicates the other person is feeling critical: hand to face, chin in palm with index finger along cheek, remaining fingers bent below the mouth. When this gesture is combined with the body drawn back from the others involved, that person is feeling critical, cynical, or in some way negative about what is being suggested or discussed. If you want someone to enlist later as an ally to *oppose* what is going on, you couldn't ask for a better prospect.

Doubt

Nose-touching or rubbing or eye-rubbing or scratching behind the ear while the person speaks often means 'No' or 'I'm not sure how you're going to react to this' or 'I'm just plain not sure'. It's often accompanied by squirming or twisting the body away. Well, now you know: the person's not sure. Sometimes, as we've noted above, it will be appropriate to stop and give them the chance to indicate what's puzzling or worrying them.

Asking for reassurance

Clenched hands with thumbs rubbing. Women often bring the hand slowly and delicately to the throat or pinch the fleshy part of the hand. If you conveniently can, provide the reassurance they're asking for and thus win their cooperation.

Of course, even if you read body-language signals accurately and respond to them, it's not always possible to solve each problem immediately. For instance, you're talking to your co-worker or boss about an assignment. Everything is progressing nicely. Abruptly she folds her arms and leans away. It's clear something is suddenly making her defensive or hostile or both. You try a different approach. You try asking questions and drawing her out. Yet this time you don't reach a clear understanding of what the irritant is. Nevertheless, your knowledge of body language has aided you. You know that something about that portion of your conversation triggered a negative reaction. You can watch for a pattern, perhaps eventually solve it.

You can also use body language in reverse. 'Body language is contagious,' says Nierenberg. 'In a circle of people put two with their hands in fists and arms folded and soon everyone will feel the need to defend themselves and you'll have fists and folded arms everywhere.' You might apply this knowledge like this: you're in an office – customer, client, or boss. As you sit there, you realise your ankles are tightly locked, you're stiff, your arms are folded tightly. Stay that way and you'll make your customer/client/boss uncomfortable and defensive with you. 'A good solution,' says Nierenberg, 'is a little internal pep talk to calm yourself and get yourself to relax. You can't fake the gestures. It has to come from the inside out. Relax and your body language will follow.'

CHAPTER **8.**

How to be more popular with your boss

Many people find it difficult to believe that bosses are real people. Oh sure, superficially they know that the boss has a home, maybe a husband or wife, children. But day in and day out they suspend the rules of ordinary common sense and tact when they deal with their own boss. Then when their thoughtless behaviour makes the boss angry, they're surprised and resentful.

You can increase your popularity with your boss enormously if you start with the assumption that bosses are human beings with much the same needs, emotions, and anxieties that you have. Like you they want to succeed at their jobs, they want their superiors to think well of them, they hate being embarrassed in public, and, if at all possible, they would like to get through each work day with a minimum of hassles.

Begin with these simple ideas and you will see that many of the things people do are guaranteed to make them *un*popular.

Who's in charge? Your boss, not you!

Your boss or your superior is in charge of the work you do because he or she is ultimately accountable for your performance. Along with this responsibility your boss is given the authority to order, direct, guide, train, and correct you in your work habits, work methods, and assignments. This may seem obvious. Yet many intelligent, even experienced people strain and eventually destroy their boss's confidence in them because they do not react positively to their boss's authority.

Bosses' success depends upon the work performance of the people, individually and collectively, reporting to them. It is the boss's job to ensure that this performance meets the prescribed company or department standards. When your behaviour and actions seem to challenge your boss's authority, *you are threatening his or her job*. How so? Your boss knows how job content and work sequence best fit in with overall plans. If a subordinate resists a supervisor's direction, individual and group work output suffer and plans go awry. Soon the boss's boss notices the unsatisfactory results. The supervisor must explain why the department is not running properly. And there it is! The supervisor can be in serious job trouble. Every boss understands and wants to prevent such a situation. Is it any wonder that bosses react strongly against subordinates if they believe their authority is being challenged?

Staying within the rules of the game

Every organisation has rules regulating employee behaviour during the workday. These may be written and publicised with penalties for violation or they may be unwritten, evolving over a period of time and generally 'understood' by everyone. Some rules may be explicit and rigid and are usually concerned with safety and security. Other rules may be flexible, subject to the inclinations of the department head or office supervisor. These are concerned with general behaviour and such things as personal time and lunch period – typically in an office where individual work is loosely related to the work of others.

Rules are necessary to ensure the welfare of the organisation and the people working there. They help supervisors and managers control and coordinate individual and group effort. They are also a guide as to where employees should and should not be during the working period. Therefore, *know the rules* of the organisation you work for. Ignorance and violation of the simplest rule could cause your boss to question your reliability and it could affect your growth potential. The violation of an explicit rule, even in ignorance, could result in any of a number of penalties, depending upon the rule violated. It could lead to a loss of a promotion opportunity, a suspension, or even a prompt termination. By keeping within 'the rules of the game', your boss will recognise that you can be trusted, that you are a solid citizen.

There are those flexible rules, the ones that seem to bend with the circumstances. Should *you* bend them to suit your convenience? Are you safe in imitating others? No. There are two things you must remember: every employee has a different personal/work history, a different subordinate/superior relationship; and your boss expects you to be where you're supposed to be during work hours.

You know that work hours are, say, nine to five with an hour for lunch. You've seen other people occasionally come in late, or extend their lunch hours, or leave a little early with no apparent repercussions. You have some urgent personal business that can be taken care of only during the day. You can handle this by extending yur lunch hour another twenty or thirty minutes. You have no urgent work assignment and are not faced with a deadline you cannot meet. What do you do? Just go to lunch and take care of your business? No! Tell your boss beforehand that you need the extra time and that your work is current. Since there is a history of work-time flexibility, the chances are your boss will say 'Go ahead.' The worst she or he may do is ask you to make up the time.

Now, what have you accomplished? You've requested permission, an acknowledgment of your boss's authority, and your boss will not go looking for you during that extra half hour with some assignment or question and become exasperated because you can't be found. What have you gained? You've made points. You've left your boss with the impression 'Here is someone I can rely upon and trust.' You can become very popular with your boss.

How far can you go without tripping?

Bosses are sensitive to their employees' behaviour, especially when they are in direct contact with them. They regard vocal tones and inflections, facial expressions, and physical posture as indications of their subordinates' attitudes *towards them*. Of course, how bosses react depends upon their personal characteristics and the existing superior/subordinate relationship. But there is a point beyond which a boss will view your attitude as a threat.

People can overstep this point by overdoing the good-natured routine. A joking, flip, or comic-sarcastic reply to work instructions or deadline requirements or about the company is overstepping. These are serious matters to your boss. You can be humorous, even kid around sometimes when the situation allows, but you must be careful not to go too far. What you want is a comfortable work relationship that projects a subtle 'Don't worry, I know you're in charge.'

Some people tend to overstep and trip because they find it difficult to accept authority. This resistance to authority, industrial psychologists say, arose in prior relationships outside the job – with parents or teachers or community officials. Without realising it, these men and women transfer their anti-authority views to the workplace. Their boss becomes the authority figure they resent. At work they project a constant chip-on-the-shoulder, hostile stance. Their work records consist of many jobs of short duration. They either go – 'I'm not going to take it from my boss any more' – or are *let* go for various legitimate reasons.

Other people who belong to ethnic, religious, or racial minorities sometimes trap themselves in the same anti-authority attitude. Those who are *super*sensitive about their cultural background may see discrimination when asked to meet legitimate job requirements. They see discrimination in the directions, in the nature of the task, as well as in the performance expected. And their reaction – a shrug, some vocal expression, dawdling, or erratic job behaviour – will be viewed as negative by their boss and they will have overstepped.

Whose way is the right way?

There is general agreement that no one has a monopoly on the best ways to do everything. It is also generally recognised that what one person sees as the 'best' way may not be the desired method or approach where several people are involved. This is usually the case when supervisors hand out assignments. How you react to assignments – how you accept them and carry them out – is another indication of your attitude toward authority.

Your boss is emphatic on how you should do a specific part of your work. You believe you can produce better results or decrease effort or time if you did the work *your* way. You explain your reasoning. Your boss brushes it aside and wants the task done 'my' way. That's it. You've made your views known. Now acknowledge your boss's authority by doing the work her/his way without foot-dragging.

Don't spend time best used for completing the assignment by trying to collect 'facts' you think will *prove* yours was the better way. Whom are you going to prove it to, your boss? It's a sure way of showing that you're challenging authority. Furthermore, you may not realise that the specified way, while not the best from your perspective, will allow for smoother coordination of your work with the work of others.

Much worse is trying to prove to your boss's boss that your ideas were better. This has the effect of your trying to show that you are more competent than your boss. Going over your superior's head is a direct attack on her/his authority and may even create the impression that your boss has lost control. Unless your proposals are extremely beneficial to company welfare or profitability or to your boss's boss, you will probably receive a cool reception from that individual. In addition you have embarrassed your boss with his/her superior. This is an unforgiveable error. You could easily be labelled a troublemaker and your boss would feel compelled to make your worklife difficult and ease you out.

Fools rush in

Not only does no one have a monopoly on good ideas, but no one is perfect. In doing your work you think your boss has erred. Are you sure it is a mistake? Are you aware of all the facts of the situation? Check. There's not a person alive who likes to be shown up. If it *is* an error, must it be brought to your superior's attention? Is your boss the only one who can correct it, or can you do so quietly? Showing your superior everything that he or she missed is a suicidal way of questioning authority, a no-win situation, and your relationship may never recover. While messengers with bad tidings are no longer beheaded, this is a highly effective way of damaging your career life.

If it is an error your boss *must* be informed about, don't point it out with 'I think you have made a mistake.' See if you can get your boss to realise it by questioning the part of the situation surrounding the error. You might try something like 'If *we* schedule the national sales rep meeting on the tenth, who should attend the new product meeting scheduled for the same day?' Since both cannot be held on the same day your boss will recognise the error. Or 'In submitting next year's departmental budget should any allocations be made for meeting rooms at the annual trade show?' The omission, if any, will be obvious. When you do try to get your supervisor to recognise an error he/she may have made, do so in private. Tell no one else in the organisation. And move cautiously. It is possible you might be in error.

Your idea – threat or acceptance

You've figured out a better method or a new approach to some programme. You are convinced it is an improvement over what now exists. How do you 'sell' your concept to your boss and see it put into effect?

Presenting any new idea to your boss involves the unspoken 'authority position'. To your boss the maintenance of the authority relationship may frequently be more important than the quality of your idea. *The only way your idea can get a fair hearing* is first to dispel any implied authority threat.

People naturally resist being manipulated. Bosses carry this natural human resistance further and surround it with suspicion of other people's intentions. If you arouse this suspicion, your boss will tend to 'decide' against your proposal in order to make it perfectly clear who is in charge. You can neutralise this suspicion. Eliminate the *I* from your opening comments. Begin with statements like 'What do you think of this idea?' or 'How does this sound to you?' Phrases like these make it clear that you know your boss is in command. You are not a threat to your boss's authority nor are you questioning his or her power to decide.

Once you've indicated your *open acceptance* of your boss's power, it doesn't have to be demonstrated to you. If your idea is sensible and your presentation is intelligent, your superior will feel comfortable in evaluating your idea on its merit. The decision will no longer be influenced by a confrontation between your boss's power to decide and your power to persuade.

Know your boss

The key to establishing a good relationship with your boss is to understand your boss's personality. What is he or she like? Ambitious or complacent? Secure or insecure? Domineering or receptive? Technically competent or feeling his or her way on the job? What does he or she consider most important as the mark of a good subordinate? Acquiescence or idea-generating? Volume of work output or quality of work? The first to arrive in the morning and the last to leave at night? Someone who keeps his or her 'nose to the grindstone' or someone who is curious about the work of others and about the company and wants to get ahead? The list can go on and on.

Develop your own list. Use it as a guide to your behaviour when dealing with your boss and how you go about your work. Set your work habits to meet what your boss looks for. If time – number of hours at work per day – is most important, put in the time. If your boss likes to hand out assignments or issue directives without any responding questions or remarks, keep your mouth shut. If you disagree with your boss's job values, get a transfer or start looking elsewhere. Your attitude will show, and whether it's a for or against attitude it will affect the way the boss responds to you.

CHAPTER 9.

Criticism and praise: why your boss treats you that way

Though it surprises them, Lynda Stacel and her mother have the same job problem. 'My boss doesn't like me,' says Lynda. 'If something goes wrong, I hear about it. But never a compliment for all the times when it's right.'

'Exactly,' says her mother. 'Remember I told you how I really pushed myself last week and got the rush work done on time. Not even a "Thank you." Where I used to work, my boss would really have appreciated it.'

After years of success at various part-time clerical jobs, Lynda and Mrs Stacel have begun working full time – as entry-level managers. Lynda finished school and is now a management trainee with a wholesale distribution company. Mrs Stacel took some college courses and won a position as an assistant branch manager of a bank.

Rosabeth Moss Kanter, an authority on human relations patterns in business organisations, suggests that Lynda and Mrs Stacel probably are worrying needlessly. In her book *Men and Women of the Corporation* (Basic Books), Dr Kanter points out that clerical and even secretarial positions arc usually dead-end occupations with relatively low salary ceilings. Because of this, bosses typically cushion the arrangement with 'a constant flow of "thanks" and compliments for jobs well done . . . love and flattery . . . roses-not-rises . . .'

When, like Lynda and Mrs Stacel, women move from clerical work to those areas of the employment world where competence can generate promotions and significant salary increases, bosses no longer feel the need to toss frequent verbal bouquets. *However, unless a woman understands this*, she may keep expecting regular doses of praise and when they're not offered may mistakenly panic and believe 'My boss doesn't like me' or, worse yet, 'I'm incompetent. My boss thinks I'm not handling this job well.'

Eleanor Brindele has a different type of problem. She really is failing at her job and her boss is running out of patience. For months he's been complaining and criticising and suggesting. No boss uses valuable time to try to guide and teach an employee unless that boss believes the employee has the basic ability to learn and succeed. But Eleanor doesn't realise this. Eleanor has changed her job performance very little. Instead of learning from the boss's comments, she steadfastly believes that her work is not the real cause of friction. 'No matter what I did he's the type that would find a reason to complain,' says Eleanor. To Eleanor the boss's many dissatisfactions represent a personality conflict, personal prejudice, or symptoms of her boss's mental health.

In Eleanor's mind each episode with her boss represents another time 'the boss picked on me' or 'the boss was letting off steam' or 'the boss doesn't really understand all the facts,' or even 'what an unreasonable man!'

Personnel Journal points out that Eleanor's is a common work error. They say many men and women eventually antagonise their bosses because subordinates often act as if they are more interested in sympathy or in fixing blame than in solving the job problems.

Kay Eaggen wishes she had a boss who would tell her straight out what is wrong. As far as Kay can judge she's doing everything humanly possible. She's prompt, accurate, hardworking. Unlike Nancy, the other young woman who was hired with her, Kay is careful not to waste time on the phone chatting with customers. Kay pleasantly takes care of business, finishes off the conversation, and gets right back to her deskwork. Yet Kay has the feeling the bosses are better pleased with Nancy than with her. 'It's not fair,' she decides.

Yet it is fair. Kay has made the crucial mistake of unilaterally deciding what is important to her job. Without realising it, Kay is seeking criticism because she has not taken the trouble to find out which work qualities her bosses consider most important. Kay has simply taken for granted that because she believes chatting with customers is considered a waste of business time, her bosses also will approve when she gets right back to her deskwork.

Kay is mistaken. Her bosses consider Kay's and Nancy's customer contacts as testing situations to determine how well they deal with people. Someone like Nancy who seems to have superior human relations skills is promoted. By minimising the time she spends with customers and maximising the time she spends on paperwork, Kay is failing to demonstrate *the kind of competence* her employers are most interested in.

Every boss has her or his own set of priorities. Job titles in themselves are meaningless. The only way Kay can succeed at this or any future job is by asking her boss a question like 'What should I be doing to make you feel I'm really good at this job?' or 'What parts of this job would you concentrate on when judging my performance?'

Then because bosses (like all human beings) may fail to give complete answers or even totally honest answers, Kay must continue to watch and listen. During the first days, as the boss explains the responsibilities, she has to notice which aspects the boss dwells on. Later, observing which incidents produce enthusiasm from the boss and which are met with indifference, she continues to learn what – on this job – represents success.

Yesterday was an amazing day at Sheryll Recca's job. At a department meeting the boss mentioned that a report Sheryll and four others had produced was 'a good job'. At lunch the five of them were incredulous. 'Do you believe it?' they kept asking each other. 'He actually gave us a compliment!'

Unfortunately, Sheryll and her colleagues' reactions are

only too common. A study reported in *Advanced Management Journal* reveals that although the average person considers 'full appreciation of work done' a top necessity, managers don't seem to have the faintest idea that non-clerical people are also interested in praise. The managers listed 'appreciation' as one of the rewards they thought people *least* desired. Money, security, promotion, and good working conditions were the only kinds of rewards managers believed that people valued.

Another study suggests that even managers who are aware of people's yearning for praise often fail to match their actions to their beliefs. Though 80 per cent of the supervisors surveyed reported they personally 'praise very often', 90 per cent of their subordinates responded 'My supervisor doesn't often show appreciation for a good job.'

The point is, of course, that even though you are starving for a bit of praise, you may be doing very well at your job. Your boss may have noticed and be fully aware of how well you're doing, and may even believe she or he has told you so! But it's a fact of life that in jobs where performance can influence advancement and salary, bosses expect high performance as a natural condition and they therefore believe not many compliments are needed.

CHAPTER 10.

Beating your 'because-I'm-a-woman' job problems

There's an ancient joke that British and American ethnic groups frequently tell on themselves – nowadays that joke probably fits working women.

It goes something like this: A man who is Italian/Jewish/ black/Irish/oriental (insert any minority you like) answers a help-wanted ad. He has an ill-fitting wooden leg, is blind in one eye, and is an eccentric who wears clothing three sizes too large for him. The ad is for a messenger who can drive a high-powered car, double-park it in central London and then sprint in and out of buildings delivering packages for a fashionable couturier. The personnel manager takes one look at this ragbag of a man who can hardly walk let alone sprint, and who because of his partial blindness cannot qualify for the driver's licence. The manager politely tells the applicant that he does not have the proper qualifications for the job. Later, reporting to his wife, the applicant says, 'The inter-viewer took one look at me, saw that I was Italian/Jewish/ black/oriental' – (insert whatever minority you wish) – 'and I didn't have a chance!'

Nowadays it seems that too many women are inserting the word 'woman'. No matter what the difficulty in obtaining a job; surviving on the job once she has it; and progressing on the job, almost every difficulty is interpreted as 'because I'm a woman'. Granted *some* difficulties may be the result of sex. Many more are probably the result of three other factors.

Recognising these three other factors can give us a more realistic understanding of what is happening to us. Since only a realistic view can produce realistic responses, it's necessary to abandon the all-purpose explanation of 'because I'm a woman' and accept the varied facets of the truth.

It's not that new understanding will eliminate all job hassles. It is rather that we will stop *misinterpreting* what's happening to us – and will then be able to *solve* many of our work-related difficulties. An experience a friend of mine had had at a top hotel during a business trip to London last winter is a perfect example. When she entered the dining room alone that evening, the *maître d'* greeted her very pleasantly and seated her. Only after she looked around did she realise (sounds like the same old story, *but wait!*) that though not near the kitchen, she was directly facing the kitchen door. She signalled the *maître d'* and asked for a better table. 'Of course,' said he and promptly and pleasantly led her to a much more desirable location.

'But then I watched,' she told me. 'The *maître d'* escorted the very next loner who entered the dining room to the table I'd left. That loner who got my abandoned table was a very prosperous looking, middle-aged businessman. The man accepted the table and remained. If I hadn't spoken up and asked for another spot, I would have eaten a miserable dinner while believing I as an unescorted woman was being discriminated against.

'But I would have been wrong! When the *maître d'* put that prosperous businessman there, it showed that he gave me the table not because I was a woman alone – but because in filling out his dining room that was the next 'singles' spot he wanted to use. *My being a woman had nothing to do with it!*'

That's the way that person behaves

Unpleasant things of all kinds can and probably do happen to all of us on the job *not* because we're women but because that's the way that person behaves. Michael Korda is only one of the perceptive social analysts who have written books chronicling the varying kinds of power ploys people use on the job. Among the many Mr Korda discusses is the habit of demonstrating power by keeping the other person waiting. The woman who has business appointments with this kind of man will find herself regularly humiliated by his I'm-more-important-than-you actions. But she will be mistaken if she sees it as a *sexual* putdown!

Not only will she be mistaken but she will be powerless to act sensibly to counter his behaviour until she accurately perceives it for what it is – a non-sexual power play that he uses with both sexes whenever he thinks he can get away with it.

A woman I know was caught in another manifestation of this personal-behaviour syndrome. She was hired as an executive with a large corporation. It appeared to be an excellent career opportunity but she soon began bewailing her problems with her male boss 'who seems to be terrified of strong, competent women'. The more hostile he grew, the more tense and angry she became. Ultimately, of course, he contrived an excuse and she was eased out. She contemplated filing an equal employment opportunity complaint. She fumed. 'A clear-cut situation of male prejudice, refusal to accept a competent woman!'

Her brother who is a lawyer asked her, 'How did your boss behave with his strong, competent *male* subordinates?'

She thought and then heard herself saying, 'There wasn't a single, strong, effective man in his department. He seems to go out of his way to hire colourless weaklings.'

Here then was a not uncommon situation where a boss cushions himself (herself) with yes-people and nonentities. His hostile reaction to her was based not on her sex but on the fact that he feels threatened by strong, competent subordinates of either sex. That's the way he behaves!

Once we comprehend that many – probably most – of the job hassles and putdowns we suffer have nothing to do with our sex, we realise we can do something about them. As long as we believe we're being slighted because of sex, we have fewer recourses. Short of legal pressures it's difficult to fight.

But once we realise that problem is caused by the other person's general behaviour patterns, we can treat it like the ordinary business or human relations situation it is. For example, a 24-year-old woman I know arrived at a hotel at 11:30 P.M. after a long business day to discover her reservation had been lost. 'All we can give you is a tiny room in the old annexe,' they told her.

Here we go, another 'businesswomen aren't important' story. Right? No, wrong. The young woman refused to believe she was a female victim and to slink away. Instead, she decided this was probably the way the clerk behaved with lost reservations of any kind, male or female. She put her brief-case on the counter, drew herself up firmly and in her best young-executive manner replied, 'I am here on business representing the XYZ company. It's not my fault my reserva-tion is lost. Hotels hold good rooms in reserve for emer-gencies. Find me one in the main building.' And within 5 minutes they did!

That's the difference we can make in what happens to us by understanding the non-sexual nature of many of our job problems and responding accordingly.

Because of the job you hold

Office politics were not invented the day you and I went to work. Neither were office politics invented in the 1970s when women in general first became serious about careers. To read the reams of advice tutoring women in office politics is only to confirm that it is a long established universal male versus male business condition.

In short, *anyone* who held the job you hold would have to deal with the office politics that accompany it. When only men held that job, the office politics was all-male warfare. Now that women also hold that job, the opposing warriors may be of opposite sexes but the warfare is not sex-provoked. It goes with the job.

An Edinburgh woman moved to a new company as a sales manager supervising seven sales people. It was soon obvious to her that two of her male subordinates were feeding her erroneous information, delaying reports she had to pass on to her supervisors, and in general attempting to discredit her. The ready-made explanation she could have used was 'They resent a woman boss'.

If she'd accepted that view, she would have squandered her time attempting to neutralise what she took to be their anxieties about working for a woman. She would have accomplished nothing except to allow them more time to discredit her.

She was fortunate enough to have a knowledgeable father. 'Find out,' he told her 'if those men tried to get themselves promoted to the sales manager job before they hired you. If they did, the men are probably not in cahoots. They're probably individually trying to get you fired. Each of them hopes that next time the company will choose from the ranks and he'll get the sales manager job.'

She investigated and sure enough, both men had applied for the sales manager position. Now with her *realistic non-sexual* appraisal of the situation, she wasted no time. She replaced the troublemakers with two new salespeople who had no preconceived antagonism against *anybody* who might be hired for the sales manager's job.

The power of any job a woman holds works both ways. It can and often does give her both the privileges and deference that the job commands as well as the jealousy and hostility it (the job itself) provokes. It's sexless. Right this minute the world is filled with frustrated male employees who have not had their contributions to their employer adequately recognised; whose careful, detailed constructive suggestions are ignored; who have been outmanoeuvred by less qualified co-workers.

When it happens to these men all of it is the result of human nature and office politics. And when the same disappointments afflict women, it also frequently is the result of human nature and office politics. Realising it, we can stop applying the one-note 'get them to accept a woman' solution to every problem. And we can get on with learning and applying the individual solutions that most of our problems require.

Because you're you and they're they

Any woman who has ever argued with the man in her life; had her own mother tell her she was behaving 'impossibly'; or had her best friend take umbrage over some word or action, should also realise that career problems are often the result of her own and others' personalities. All of us sometimes fight with our nearest and dearest. Other times we radiate fury silently. Whatever the ways of expressing cross purposes and anger, nobody's personal life is 100 per cent peaceful. Why then should we expect that working in close harness with strangers 8 hours a day, 5 days a week should be frictionless?

When it turns out not to be frictionless, again the answer is not that they're having trouble relating to us as female co-workers. The problem more likely is caused by the two of us rubbing each other the wrong way as human beings.

Much of the conflict is predictable. For instance, Dr Andrew H. Souerwine, management consultant and professor of management at the University of Connecticut graduate school of business, has analysed various boss personality types. Each of the types reacts favourably to subordinates and other co-workers who display particular behaviour patterns and reacts with disapproval to other behaviour patterns. *The sex of the subordinates or bosses are not the triggers. It is a matter of the varying personality types involved.*

Though no one is totally any type, Dr Souerwine points out that every supervisor emphasizes one style and anyone who understands this can *foresee* which kinds of subordinates' behaviour (regardless of sex) will succeed, which will fail. Some highlights that can be foreseen include: the action-oriented supervisor who wants his subordinates to arrive at a meeting with completely thought-out ideas and never takes kindly to the careful worker who suggests, 'Let's just discuss it and see where it takes us.' This type is also deadly when anyone seems to ignore the boss's authority or keeps information back.

Then there's the security-oriented boss who wants a standardised operating system for everything. Sex of the employee has nothing to do with it when this boss panics and blasts the subordinate who sets herself (or himself) up as getting results by fighting or going around the system.

With the idea-oriented boss, the gung-ho subordinate of either sex who presses to get things moving without lengthy study and consideration of a maze of possibilities is asking for trouble. (Though the action-oriented boss would have loved her/him.)

Obviously all these personality types will not only produce boss-subordinate conflict but will also cause dissension when personality-anti-types are harnessed together as peers supposedly working together. They are human beings who see life differently. Differences of temperament, not sexual differences, will be the explanation for their controversies.

After college I spent my first year teaching in a state school. That was years ago and the principal was one of that now vanished group of spinsters who devoted their lives to teaching. She was close to retirement and though I chafed under many of her ways, she taught me a great deal about human nature.

Once when she reprimanded me for being 'a careless person' who hastened through some of the boring school paperwork, I protested that 'I'm not careless about paperwork in personal life.'

'That can't be true,' she said in her forthright way. 'Nobody is two people. Whoever you are in your personal life shows up in your work life.'

And of course, she was right. About all of us.

Whatever we do that irritates people in our private life will almost surely show up and produce discord on the job. But it will not be controversy born of the fact that we're females. It'll be the result of who we are and of who the other person is.

In short, they won't be female-male antagonisms unless we mistakenly twist them out of shape into sexual battles. No, they'll just be human being problems.

In understanding the universal *sexless* nature of most of our job conflicts, lies our ability to analyse them and cope.

PART III

MORE MONEY, MORE FRINGE BENEFITS, MORE JOB RIGHTS

CHAPTER 11.

How to get more money from your job fringe benefits

It's two hours past five-thirty. Norma is finally finished. She signs off her computer terminal and looks at the clock with satisfaction as she mentally adds her two hours of overtime pay to her weekly paycheque. Across town in another office, working for another company, Carole is also completing two hours of overtime at her terminal. As she leaves she has no pleasant thought of extra pay. She never earns anything for overtime work. Elsewhere in the same city Gloria and Jeanette are office supervisors, doing similar work for two different employers. When Gloria spends extra time at her desk, it means extra income. When Jeanette stays late, her boss says 'Thank you' (if he remembers) and that's that.

The same pattern repeats itself for women (and men too) who hold other kinds of white-collar, professional, and technical positions, such as personnel people, office workers, accountants, engineers, scientific workers, product designers, and the like. Some draw sizeable overtime fringe incomes while others who are in essentially identical jobs earn nothing for longer hours.

Multiply it week after week, month after month, year after year and the difference in the overtime and no-overtime income can influence your entire standard of living. Being able to splurge on an exciting vacation, afford the housing you'd really like, buy the kind of clothes you want, build savings and investments, can all depend on your obtaining the most not only from your overtime possibilities but from all your other potential fringe income.

Receiving the most from your benefits depends on the geographic area of Britain you work in, the industry you work in, seeing to it that your extras keep pace with inflation and your responsibilities, and knowing what to request.

Use the information in this chapter to:

- appraise your present job
- ask questions during future job interviews
- judge the overall potential income of your present job or of a new job offer
- obtain new benefits at your present job
- enlarge your current benefits package

How can you put the last two items into action? If after reading this chapter you realise that the people with your kind of job *do* enjoy a particular benefit, you can bring the fact tactfully to your employer's attention. If you are the only individual at your company doing your kind of job (for example, the only public relations person, the only office manager, the only purchasing expediter) you may find that persuading management to add you to the employees who receive one or more extra fringe benefits is relatively easy. Because you are the only individual holding your kind of position, your employers will not worry about setting a precedent that will cause others to demand the same. If they are pleased with your work, they may feel it is an excellent and for them a relatively inexpensive way to reward you.

When a group of you work at the same kinds of tasks, representatives of your group should bring the request to management's attention. For example health insurance is a rapidly growing but relatively new kind of extra.

In a small organisation your group's chances of having health insurance added to your benefits package rise if you gather some of the preliminary information. Before asking your company to add private medical insurance coverage,

77

find out the names of the two or three largest companies offering such insurance (use the telephone Yellow Pages, if necessary) and contact them. Ask them to send details of the schemes they offer for groups of employees to you.

If you belong to a white-collar trade union, you can ask its information division to give you details of the kinds of benefits enjoyed by employees in other, similar, firms to yours. Your company is more likely to agree to extra benefits if you can prove that they need to do so to stay competitive.

By handing this packet of basic information to your employer when you make your request, you overcome much of the initial inertia. In a small organisation, there is a very limited personnel staff. Because your boss doesn't face time-consuming research, you've made it easy for those in charge to follow up and obtain the complete information they need to consider and perhaps agree to the new benefits.

Is this realistic?

Yes. Don't underestimate your influence by thinking 'What can I and a few friends accomplish in this big company?' The Conference Board, a respected business research organisation, reports that the average company is continuously adding provisions and underlying policies that change its whole benefits package. The Administrative Management Society, another important business research organisation, agrees, saying that 'the scope of benefits is constantly expanding'.

Where you work

In general, the larger the company the more benefits you receive. Certain types of job attract more benefits than others; banks pay high benefits; so do sales jobs. Companies which are relocating out of London to areas like Wales or the North East may offer additional benefits to people willing to go there.

Does it go with your job

Sometimes people feel their job isn't important enough to merit something like an incentive bonus. Other times they accidentally cheat themselves because they think their jobs are too important. They think white-collar, professional, or technical people like themselves shouldn't expect something like a clothing allowance or other extras they associate with hourly workers.

Check your expectations of what you could be getting against these facts:

Incentive plans

Contrary to popular impression, this is not a top-management preserve. Two out of three companies that provide the plans to top management also include some people in more modest jobs in middle management – and if you supervise even a few people, you are probably a part of middle management. If you're not now part of your company's incentive programme that rewards you with extra pay for extra results, ask to be included. But never allow your employer to substitute an incentive bonus for a pay increase. A pay increase is a permanent part of your salary record and will aid you if you change jobs. A bonus is an annual 'maybe'. Besides, surveys reveal that base salaries for bonus and non-bonus jobs are often the same. This means that if a non-bonus company pays £10,000 annually for your kind of job, the bonus-paying organisation is probably also paying a £10,000 base *and then adding* the bonus or profit sharing.

Your expense account

Sometimes a little ingenuity brings you expenses privileges. A London woman started calling some of the company's European customers from her home at 7:00 A.M. her time, 9:00 A.M. their time. She had no expense account, and when she asked to be reimbursed for the calls her boss was annoyed. 'Why are you so inefficient you have to take work home?' he asked her.

She had her answer ready. 'I purposely do the calls on my own time because I've discovered people I have to talk to are always available then. I get more accomplished for us that way.' The boss listened, approved the expenses, and seemed impressed with her initiative. She's steadily increasing the list of items she is authorised to charge. Last week it was more than £60 for three useful professional publications she's formerly subscribed to with her own funds.

Sometimes you have an expense account and stretching your privileges depends on speaking out and changing your boss's mind. One young woman whose work required considerable travel had her long-distance phone calls to her boyfriend rejected as 'personal recreation'. When she pointed out that the company was willing to pay for the 'personal recreation' of some of her male colleagues when they listed prostitutes on their expenses as 'entertainment', her phone calls were permanently approved.

Many woman err in the other direction. They make the mistake of conscientiously pinching pennies for their employer. And their bosses think *less* of them for it. One sales representative was fortunate in having an outspoken superior who called her in after three months and told her 'I don't believe these lunch expenses. You can't be doing your job right if you're taking clients to such two-bit restaurants. And why is so little spent on prospective clients for meals and entertainment?'

Saving taxi fares by taking buses can be another error. If your job is important enough to merit an expense account, you shouldn't be wasting precious minutes and hours during business time getting from here to there by bus.

Holidays

You might prefer a long holiday abroad next year to a short holiday this year. Some companies will agree to carry over a portion of this year's leave and add it to your allowance for next year. Ask. Want to change jobs but feeling gloomy about losing your chance for a holiday with pay this year? Check with your new employer; many will allow you at least some annual leave after you have worked there for at least three months, and some will agree to your taking an already planned holiday even sooner, so long as you discuss it with them when taking the job. And, of course, the firm you worked for previously has to give you extra pay in lieu of any holiday entitlement you did not take before you left.

Overall

Some of the popular fringe benefits people in jobs like yours are receiving:

- paid study leave for you to get extra qualifications (and the company may pay any fees, etc.)
- luncheon vouchers or subsidised canteen meals
- a discount on goods or services purchased from the company
- use of a company car
- private medical insurance premiums
- clothing allowances
- pension schemes.

CHAPTER **12.**

How to find out what other people with your job make

Friends who will tell you the most intimate secrets of their emotional and sexual lives hesitate and usually draw the line at revealing their salaries. Discussing money, sociologists explain, is one of the last taboos. This leaves you with no real way of knowing if you're receiving low, average, or excellent income for the type of work you do.

Should you pull yourself out of your inertia and go job-hunting because you're poorly compensated and could easily better yourself? Or are you receiving top pay and unusual extras without realising it?

There are some ways to find out. One is to look at the job vacancies advertised in the newspapers, and try to find the salary range for jobs like yours. Don't get carried away by a few exceptional offers: look at what the majority of firms are offering for similar work, and what fringe benefits are included.

For example, a few advertisements for a Public Relations Officer may include a salalry of £15,000 or more. But if most of the companies are offering around £9,000 then the few exceptions are probably advertisements for a quite different level of responsibility and experience – even if the job has the same name. Be realistic about which category you belong to –

think in terms of which posts you could apply for as alternatives to the one you have now, rather than ones which would be a promotion.

Alternatively, you may belong to a union which can advise you on the kinds of pay and benefits which its other members in similar jobs are getting.

Once you obtain the facts, you can at last judge your current situation. As you do so, you should also weigh what the intangible advantages of your job are worth to you. Maybe you've discovered your salary is only average for your area, but you can walk to work and management is flexible about the personal time you sometimes need. Or perhaps you're acquiring valuable skills and there is good opportunity for advancement. Depending on your own values, various combinations of average salary plus various intangibles can add up to an above-average remuneration package from your viewpoint.

As you consider the comparative salary information, you also have to be realistic about yourself. What sort of an employee are you? Average? Above average? Are you still learning your job? You can't expect to earn top income if your performance is mediocre or if you have limited experience. But suppose, after considering everything and with your new salary knowledge, you do believe you merit a rise. The facts you've obtained can be a valuable tool. But they're not a magic incantation. You must go on using the same tact and common sense you would have used in the past.

Merely to ask for an increase because the average pay in your area is more than you're earning can lead to a quick refusal because this is probably what your company is accustomed to paying. Instead, at an appropriate time you must review with your boss all the job-related reasons – performance, experience, responsibility, etc. – that indicate you are competent. If your boss agrees that you are a valued employee, then it's time to indicate the increase you want, using the survey data (bring them with you) to support your request. Your boss has just agreed that you are competent. It's now going to seem logical to her or him to pay the going rate for competent employees for your area.

You can also use the salary and fringe benefits information to help you decide about the long-distance move you may have been contemplating. Allowing for cost-of-living differences, will you be able to duplicate or improve your career situation? Many organisations (including the Civil Service) offer a special London Weighting for those working within Greater London: it is seldom enough, however, to cover the extra costs of housing, travel and so on.

CHAPTER 13.

The truth about women's salaries – and how it can help you earn more

MYTH 1
Government statistics prove that the average woman in Britain earns only about 74 pence for every pound earned by the average British male.

MYTH 2
Any real difference in the amount of money the average woman earns as compared to what the average man earns is the result of discrimination.

MYTH 3
Men are starting to move into so-called women's occupations like nursing and secretarial work and naturally they will get the best jobs and further depress women's salaries.

Myth 1

It doesn't matter how many times or in how many prestige publications you've read that the average woman worker in Britain earns only three-quarters of what the average man gets. *It isn't true.*

The oft-quoted statistic, which might mistakenly discourage you, is a perfect example of how statistics can sound important but really mean almost nothing.

Why then the confusion and why the widespread use of this statistic? The answer lies in the way the government, which provides the statistic, gathers and computes its data. For your protection you should know the facts. *With this knowledge you can then choose your area of work and know that, when doing it, you will usually be earning what you deserve.*

First, the statistic is universally used because the government statisticians compute it from the New Earnings Survey and publish it in the *Employment Gazette*, from which the press and others print and quote it without bothering to define how the statistic is arrived at.

It is the *how* that makes the statistic so misleading and ultimately meaningless. The first misleading part lies in the word *average*: as in 'the average male worker earns a pound for every 74 pence earned by the average female worker'.

It works like this. Say we have three employed men. One man makes £8,000 a year; the second man earns £12,000, and the third man is president of his own company and pays himself £100,000 a year. To find the average, we add up the three salaries (£8,000, £12,000 and £100,000) and then divide by three. When we finish our arithmetic, we have £40,000 as the average salary for the three men. Impressive, isn't it, the way that one man with his £100,000 salary really pulls up the average? It makes those two men at lowly £8,000 and £12,000 look grand.

This is exactly what happens when the government works out the average for all men's salaries and all women's salaries.

Most of the people who are presidents of companies or top executives are men (but relatively a very small group of men). The government adds in the small group of men with huge salaries and the total men's 'average' jumps skyward. But it's a false impression. The average man is still making his £8,000 or £11,000 or £16,000 just as women are. The difference lies in the fact that there is not yet a significant group of prosperous women business owners and top executives to push up the average of women's salaries.

Where the statistics include overtime pay, the distortion is even greater, because men work far more overtime than women. So, in 1982 women's full-time gross weekly earnings, including the effects of overtime, averaged only 66 per cent of men's.

On other occasions government statistics are given as the 'median' salary. When this happened recently, it was announced that women's median salary is now lower than before women's liberation. The media faithfully transmitted this announcement without analysing or explaining how meaningless it was. People everywhere not understanding the cause of the statistic (and therefore not realising it was meaningless) wrote 'knowledgeable' newspaper editorials and magazine articles discussing how women were falling even further behind in the salary struggle. The articles, like the statistic, were useless.

Here's why. The median is found by going to the exact middle of a list. For example, five salaries: £20,000, £18,000, £10,000, £9,000 and £4,000. The median here is £10,000, the salary in the middle of the list. Because of liberation, millions of middle-aged women with inadequate job preparation have flooded the job market. There they take unimpressive-entry-level jobs at unimpressive entry-level salaries. Previously there had been only two groups of women in the job market: those who had to work and often did so at unskilled low-level salaries and a relatively large group of professional women (teachers, nurses, secretaries) whose modest but professional salaries lifted the unskilled-labour salaries.

Now with the new millions of unskilled women jamming the work market, the low end of the women's list is lengthened. The statistician looking for the median thus finds it down in the low end of women's salaries. But this median in no way reflects what trained female workers are asking and receiving in salaries. The truth, of course, is that women with training have never had so many opportunities. Nor have so many of them ever earned as much as they are now earning.

A third kind of meaningless government statistic that can mistakenly discourage you is the one that shows that young male college graduates' starting salaries are markedly higher than starting salaries for female college graduates. Again, no real meaning – or problem.

Most of the women college graduates still enter occupations like teacher, therapist, librarian, nurse, social worker, where salaries, *regardless of sex*, are modest. Most male college graduates enter professions or move into business, where entry-level salaries are higher. There's still another kind of statistic (produced by various research groups) that is as meaningless as the government's statistics. This one sounds really discouraging. There's this 45-year-old Oxford graduate earning £25,000 a year while his wife (or some other woman), who is also forty-five and an Oxford graduate, is earning £8,000 a year.

Now doesn't that prove the hopelessness of the salary disparity? No, it doesn't. If you look at that example – and any other similar examples you come across – you will find that there is never any mention of whether the two people have an equal number of *un*interrupted working years behind them. Nowhere do these comparisons ever note that he has been working for twenty-five uninterrupted years at high-income occupation to reach his £25,000 salary level while she has taken a number of years off (sometimes as many as twenty or more) to bear and raise a family and is now engaged in an occupation that pays low salaries.

Overall then, the only salary statistic that means anything at all in this male-female comparison is the one that reports whether women are earning comparable pay for comparable work and comparable *uninterrupted* years of experience of training. *These statistics for comparable people in comparable jobs are virtually nonexistent.*

Myth 2

Most women who have trouble finding jobs that pay well are not victims of discrimination. They are victims of their own choices. They *voluntarily* (though often out of ignorance) confine their career choices and their job-hunting to low-paying occupations. Once you understand this you can stop confining yourself to the 'glamour' industries and the 'female ghetto' industries. You can move quickly into vastly better-paying jobs by making different choices. It's up to you.

Glamour industries

The so-called glamour occupations are those such as the travel industry, fashion, recreation, communication. Because so many capable young people of both sexes are anxious to work in these industries top-grade staff can be hired for very modest wages. In publishing, for instance, new college graduates working as editorial assistants are paid a sum that is often less than that paid to good clerical workers.

However, many women (and men too) are satisfied to make this economic trade-off to establish themselves in one of these 'exciting' careers. Only you can decide whether it is the correct choice for you. But whatever you decide, remember your low salary is not the result of your sex or of discrimination. It is the result of the industry you choose.

Many other young women are frustrated by relatively low salary opportunities because they job-hunt only in what have been labelled the 'female ghetto' industries, the occupations traditionally considered 'women's work'. Occupations like librarian, beautician, secretary, and nursery-school teacher fall into this category. These careers are still suffering from the low salary ceilings women's work has traditionally offered. Under these old established ways of judging the value of 'women's work' we have the typical situation where a town pays one of its garbage collectors more than it pays a woman who daily teaches and guides a nursery-school class of human beings.

During the 1980s the women's movement is mounting a campaign to re-evaluate 'women's jobs' and establish higher, more realistic wage scales to compensate for the real value of the work. Watch for ways to support the comparable work effort. But meanwhile, if you are in a hurry to make more money, some of the better-paying occupations include accountancy, computer science, engineering, sales and marketing.

The most valuable lifetime investment you might make in yourself is obtaining the training to fit you for one of these well-paying jobs. Even if you have to use a bank loan to support you while you study, these occupations will enable you to repay quickly once you begin working.

Myth 3

Because of the widespread shortage of secretaries and because of equal-opportunity laws, many companies are putting men behind secretarial desks. In America, AT&T has 13,200 male secretaries, 12.3 per cent of its total. Kelly Services Inc. in Boston says that about 10 per cent of its clerical workers are males. In Britain this development is somewhat slower but it is beginning to happen. Some of the new male secretaries complain about hostility from female secretaries, who resent them. Women call it 'sexist' if men hesitate to accept women when they work in traditionally male occupations. Women rejecting male secretaries is the same intolerant behaviour, only now women are doing the harassing.

In addition to the justice of accepting the male secretary as an individual rather than judging him by his sex, *it will probably benefit all women to have men in these jobs*. Clerical and secretarial salaries in general will probably rise. Other so-called women's occupations reveal a pattern of rising salaries – for both men and women – as the occupations leave the all-women image behind and become female-male occupations.

CHAPTER **14.**

The truth about your job rights

Once you know what you are entitled to it's often easy to get it. It's not knowing that keeps you immobilised with worries of 'What will happen if I do that?', 'Can I do that?', and 'Can they really do this to me?'

Salary talk

When you were hired, the personnel department or your boss indicated you were being paid a little more than other people and warned you not to discuss your salary with others because such discussions were against company policy.

Since then it has occurred to you that perhaps they manipulate everyone away from discussing salaries by suggesting that everyone's extra-privileged. With the no-discussion policy it is difficult to find out.

Many companies have had policies like your employer's. Some have warned employees they would be fired for violating the rule. Others ensure employee submission just by spreading the word that 'Management won't like it' or 'You'll make trouble for yourself if you tell others what you earn.'

If you inquire, companies often explain that this rule eliminates resentment among employees receiving different salaries for doing similar tasks. What it really does is protect unfair salary practices.

The company has no legal right to stop employees discussing salaries. And, while a company is not bound to disclose individual salaries, a staff association or union can ask the company to list the numbers of employees on different grades or in certain salary ranges – and to include a sex breakdown. From that information you can work out whether people in the same levels of work as you are being graded and paid at roughly similar levels or not.

Must the person with seniority get the promotion?

One of the biggest problems facing working women today is their relatively short time on the job. When promotion possibilities open up in the office, store, or factory, the women are often at a disadvantage because they haven't been on the job as long as most of the men.

One way round this is if your company has job-selection tests (and more and more of them do). If job-selection tests are used, and have been accepted as really measuring the kinds of skills needed to succeed at that job, then the newer employee has just as good a chance at proving she can do the work.

Another alternative is the Sex Discrimination Act. Where a requirement applies to men and women alike, but the proportion of each who can comply with it is much smaller there may be indirect discrimination. You would have to prove that this was a real disadvantage and not justifiable irrespective of sex. For example, if an employer made it a condition of promotion that the employee had to have five years' experience, but had only taken on women workers in the past three years, you would have a good case. It is always worth investigating.

One woman succeeded in a claim against the Post Office when she was not given a postman's 'walk' because her previous experience as a postwoman did not count until 1969 – before then, only a post*man*'s previous service counted.

Access to their records

It's your body. And your company requires you to take that body to the company's medical office and submit it to a regular physical examination. 'For your own good,' they tell you. Then they make it difficult – if not impossible – for you to find out exactly what they are reporting about you in those medical records. It's a common problem and the answer is not very satisfactory. Under English law a patient has no absolute legal right to information about her case, and no access to medical files. Your employer commissions the doctor to report on you and the report belongs to the employer.

You may refuse to consent to the examination – but if your employment contract obliges you to have a medical examination the company has grounds for dismissing you if you don't comply. Alternatively, you can ask that a copy of the report by the company doctor is sent to your own doctor, and just hope he is willing to tell you what is in it or to show it to you.

Pregnancy

The law protects people who are dismissed because they are pregnant or for any reason to do with their pregnancy, provided they have been employed by the same employer for at least 12 months before the dismissal. So you would be covered not just while pregnant, but if you had a miscarriage or a boss who disapproved of single parenthood. If you have worked in the same place for less than 12 months you may be covered under the Sex Discrimination Act.

You could be dismissed, though, if you could not do your normal work properly when pregnant, or if there were legal provisions forbidding somebody to employ you (for instance, where the work involves radiation exposure). In both cases the employer has to prove there is no alternative work you can be offered. (And you are still entitled to maternity pay and to go back to the job after maternity leave – when your service will be regarded as unbroken, just as it is for other pregnant women.)

You are entitled to paid time off for ante-natal checkups and other medical reasons to do with the pregnancy. And, if you have worked for the same employer for at least 2 years, 11 weeks before the baby is expected to be born you are entitled to claim maternity leave and pay. The minimum maternity leave with pay which your employer must offer you is 6 weeks at 90 per cent of your salary (less the State maternity allowance). Many part-time workers are excluded from this benefit, though. Some firms offer better conditions than these legal minimums: if you are planning a family in the foreseeable future, you should look carefully at maternity provision in the fringe benefits you are being offered by any company.

Keeping the job after pregnancy

You have the right to go back to work for the same organisation and in the same or an equivalent job after pregnancy leave – but *you must tell your employer*, in writing, at least 3 weeks before you go on leave, that you intend to come back and when the birth is expected.

If you change your mind and decide after the baby is born that you will stay at home, your employer can't make you pay back the maternity pay, or penalise you in any way.

Maternity leave does not affect your continuity of service when it comes to things like redundancy pay – but it may not qualify you for holiday earned during the period, or for your company's pension scheme. Again, check the benefits that individual companies are offering.

You must return to your job within 29 weeks from the birth, although it is possible for medical reasons to delay return for another 4 weeks, with a medical certificate.

The regulations about pregnancy and pregnancy leave and pay are complicated and they are made more complicated by the variety of extra arrangements different companies offer. This is only a general outline; check on the details through your public library, Citizens' Advice Bureau, union or similar source.

Can you keep pregnancy a secret?

Suppose your pregnancy problem is just the opposite. Rather than receiving health and other benefits because of your pregnancy, you're anxious to keep your pregnancy a secret as long as you can. Many women want to delay telling their boss lest they be passed over for promotion or a rise because the boss fears (rightly or wrongly) that the woman will soon be giving notice or asking for a leave of absence. Must you tell your boss as soon as you know you are pregnant?

In order to qualify for maternity leave, and to be able to get your job back afterwards, you must write to your employer at least 3 weeks before you begin maternity leave. You can decide when to take maternity leave but if you leave *earlier* than 11 weeks before the expected birth, you won't get maternity pay and leave (unless you are unwell and are on sick leave). You can go on working as long as you wish unless the pregnancy means you can't do your job adequately.

Can your children be a handicap in getting a job?

If you are refused a job, or treated less favourably by an employer, because you have children it counts as both direct and indirect discrimination under the Sex Discrimination Act. No employer has the right to say that he won't take on or promote women with children because they are less reliable or hardworking. Unless the company applies the same policy to men it is practising direct discrimination. And it is indirect discrimination to say that all women are unreliable when they have children to look after; the firm must investigate each case separately.

Does income tax have to be discriminatory?

For tax purposes, a married woman's income belongs to her husband. He is assessed on the joint income; is responsible for making the declaration of income to the Inland Revenue; is responsible for paying any tax due; and usually gets any rebate owing. So if you have been overtaxed at work, he will usually get the cheque.

This outrageous system has made a lot of people angry for years. There are proposals around for changing it, but not very much. So, until there is some really radical reform of the tax system, there are only two limited options open to a working married woman.

Separate assessment
Either partner can apply for this, and only one signature is needed on the form. The effect is that each partner is liable for tax on his or her own income. Each may complete an income tax declaration. The Married Man's Allowance is split between the two in the proportion of their incomes. It does not affect the couple's total tax bill, or the existence of the higher Married Man's Allowance.

Wife's earned income assessment
Both husband and wife have to apply for this and sign the form. All joint income is declared on one joint tax return, under the husband's signature. The husband then gets a single person's allowance instead of the married man's one which would be higher; his wife also gets a single person's allowance instead of the (identical) wife's earned income allowance. She is responsible for paying tax on her earned income, and gets any benefits due, *but* any unearned income (savings, investments, etc.) is still regarded as her husband's, and he pays tax on it. Because this option reduces the man's tax allowance, it is only worthwhile if the couples have a joint income which puts them in the higher tax brackets. In those instances, two separate assessments can reduce the tax bill.

Tax and allowances are extremely complicated and this is only a very general outline of what happens to a married woman's earnings. For more specialist help, the Consumers' Association publish a very good *Tax Guide*.

Social Security

Provided you are earning more than £32.50 a week, you will have to pay a National Insurance contribution of 9 per cent of your salary up to an upper earnings limit. Your employer also has to pay £11.95 per cent of your salary in National Insurance contributions. If your company has its own approved occupational pension scheme which has 'contracted out' of the State scheme, both your own and your employer's contributions to the National Insurance scheme will be reduced. But, of course, some of your salary will be going into the occupational pension scheme as well, and your employer will also be contributing to it.

At one time, when you got married you could decide whether to go on paying the full National Insurance contribution, or a reduced married woman's contribution which entitled you to fewer benefits. This alternative is now being phased out.

If you move jobs fairly frequently, it still may be worth subscribing to a company's occupational pension scheme, if only as a way of acquiring some savings. When you leave, you can take out all your (but not the employer's) contributions so long as you have been working with the organisation for less than 5 years. Alternatively, you can try to transfer the pension to your new company's scheme – some are transferable – or leave it where it is, knowing that eventually you will get a bit of pension from that company based on both your and the employer's contributions.

Pension schemes are complicated and difficult to understand and you may need to get advice from a specialist, such as the firm's accountant or your bank manager. There is a good basic financial guide published by the Women's Institute, called *Money Matters for Women* by Liz McDonnell (Willow Books, Collins).

PART IV
TROUBLE!

CHAPTER 15

Boss troubles and how to deal with them

The constant criticiser

Your boss has developed the habit of picking on you. You are criticised in private and even in public. You are as competent a worker as anyone else and you know you're just as nice a person. Why pick on you?

You've been chosen to be the victim because your reactions are providing your boss with a malicious kind of fun, says Paula Kurman, formerly professor of communication at Hunter College and now a consultant to industry. Dr Kurman, who specialises in the structure of interpersonal relations, also worked with Margaret Mead on various human relations research projects. Dr Kurman explains that to change the situation *quickly* you must recognise and then alter the ways you are contributing to your problem. Most people refuse at first to believe they are in any way provoking the torment. 'It's easier to blame the other person,' says Dr Kurman. 'But you can stop people from picking on you by changing your part in the game, by abandoning the defence posture you've unconsciously adopted. Since people form communication systems that interlock, when you change your part, the other person *has to* change his or hers.

You may already have experimented with all the typical reactions. You've defended yourself and your work many times. You've had a quiet talk with your boss exploring the reasons for his or her behaviour. You've tried ignoring it. You may have tried counterattacking – 'If that's the way you're going to behave, I can act that way too.' Nothing has worked.

They never will work, according to Dr Kurman, because they are all ways of defending yourself. The only solution is to get out of your defence posture. 'Then you will leave the attacker alone in the fight ring. You can't have a fight with one fighter. The game/fight has to stop.'

You initially change the situation by recognising your attacker's real motives. 'There's a difference between occasional constructive criticism and regular sessions of harassment,' says Dr Kurman. 'Bosses who harass do so not because they are strong but because they're weak. They're really yelling "insecurity". Do you know anyone who is strong and "together" who goes around bullying people? All the defence reactions you've tried have increased *your attacker's sense of insecurity and vulnerability*. You've had this effect by trying to disprove whatever they're asserting. It's important for you to know you're facing fear and weakness. It takes the pressure off the vulnerability we each carry with us and permits you to use different, more constructive methods. Now you are able to break the pattern.'

You break the pattern by 'reframing' the situation, by putting it in a different light. First, understand your own reaction pattern. Dr Kurman helps her clients do this by asking them 'If you had to write what usually happens for a TV script, exactly step-by-step how would it go?'

'Well, I walk in carrying the papers and then . . .'

Says Dr Kurman, 'When they stop to think of it, people always know their repetitive script. Now they must change it. Exactly how *you* accomplish it depends on what you are comfortable with. But realise, just the fact that you now intend to be helpful rather than hostile and defensive alters the way you look, walk, stand, move when you're with your boss. Eighty per cent of all communication is done with the body, not with words. Just coming to work with your new attitude has already metamorphosed the total atmosphere between you and your superior.'

Many people (men fall into the victim role as frequently as women) have extricated themselves by deciding that at the next outburst they're going to treat their insecure boss in a new way. They're going to say something to the effect of 'You know, I've been thinking it over. You're really trying to help me. I really appreciate it. Thank you for your interest.' Should there be a second or third attack, by following your new script of not fighting back your boss is left battling the air. But often there isn't more than one explosion. The victim's new relaxed attitude during the attack and thereafter make clear she has stopped fighting. She has reframed the situation, telling her attacker that he's a good guy who is making her stronger. She's taken the fun out of it. Her attacker will soon go off in search of someone who will fight back and who can be 'conquered'.

Whenever you're being picked on, you also have to consider the possibility you are subconsciously seeking various payoffs. Dr Kurman points out that people always transfer their victim behaviour back and forth from their work to their private life. Many people, for example, who grew up as the victim child in the family, the one who was clumsy or frail or somehow the 'poor thing', go on looking for opportunities to play the same poor-thing role in life and in their work. Then they can keep talking about 'how dreadfully I'm treated' and go on lapping up the sympathy. Other women with whom Dr Kurman has worked have twisted women's liberation's excellent ideas into hostile chips on their shoulders. They repeatedly alienate their bosses and get themselves fired. This is the payoff they're often unwittingly seeking. Now they won't ever have to find out if they're truly competent. They won't ever have to face the challenges of success. They can go on blaming the system.

Paula Lurman advises that after you understand your personal victim script you stay at your present job for a few months. Practise observing and reframing. People often discover with their new constructive attitude, new knowledge, and new behaviour that at the end of the practice months they don't have to leave. They're happy where they are.

When your boss spreads written criticism about you

Your boss found some critical comments about you in your personnel file written by a previous boss of yours who never liked you. Your present boss showed the comments to the company vice-president, who then denied you a rise because of them. Does your boss have the right to distribute old unfavourable items from your file?

It all depends. Your boss has the legal right to circulate criticism of you *only* to people in your organisation who have a role in evaluating your work. Because the vice-president used the information to decide about a rise, this was a legitimate action by your supervisor. However, your boss cannot disseminate the negative remarks to other co-workers or executives. If she or he does, you could sue and probably win.

If you realise that you have made some significant mistakes at your present job, your best course is to change jobs and leave those critical facts and reports behind you. Nowadays, employers aware of the many lawsuits employees have won on this point have become very cautious. Few employers (if any) will pass on negative work-assessment information to your new employer since they fear it would open your old firm to a lawsuit by you.

When you really are being discriminated against

Your employer cannot use the fact that you are a woman to refuse you a job, pass over you for promotion, pay you less than a man is paid for similar work. (Neither can you be discriminated against because of your colour, race, or country of origin.)

If you believe that you have been the victim of illegal discrimination in any form, you can get in touch with the Equal Opportunities Commission. It was established by the Equal Opportunities Act, to help enforce the law and promote equality of opportunity between the sexes. It offers information and advice to the general public and in some cases can assist individuals who think they have been discriminated against.

Its address is: Equal Opportunities Commission, Overseas House, Quay Street, Manchester M3 3HN (telephone 061–833 9244). Among its publications are a *Guide to the Sex Discrimination Act*, which sets out what the law actually says, and standard forms which a person thinking she may be a victim of discrimination can use to decide whether she has a case and if so how to put it effectively. These forms are available both from the EOC and from employment offices and job-centres and from unemployment benefit offices.

Complaints about discrimination in employment are dealt with by industrial tribunals. You can't get Legal Aid for the hearing, but if your income is below a certain level you can get legal advice and help from a solicitor up to a value of £40. If you need legal help it is best to talk first to your local Citizens' Advice Bureau. If you belong to a trades union the union may help you to present the case to the tribunal. Generally, a complaint to an industrial tribunal has to be made within 3 months of whatever it was you are objecting to. If the tribunal finds in your favour, it may order that you be paid damages or it may recommend that you should be reinstated, or considered for promotion, or promoted, for example.

CHAPTER 16.

Which kind of boss do you have?

Yesterday as usual, Diane's boss called her in, shot a few directions at her and ordered, 'Get right on it. I want it by Friday.' As happens so often lately, Diane went home with a tension-headache. As soon as the economy improves and job opportunities rise, she's planning to change jobs. Diane's boss pushes constantly, allows no time for evaluation or methods or goals, and wants everything done 'now'. Once Diane actually challenged him. 'But first, wouldn't it be worthwhile to consider this from various angles?' she asked. 'We might end up with better results.'

Her boss flicked her an impatient look. 'Just get it done', he said.

It's not surprising that Diane's work days make her tense and nervous. She has the wrong kind of boss for her. Because she has an idea-oriented personality, it makes her very uncomfortable to leap into action without first studying the situation. If she could find an idea-oriented boss, that supervisor would be pleasant for her to work with. Both of them would agree to slow down and look for the best solution, the best method.

But Diane's current boss is the exact opposite. He is action-oriented. A very common type of boss – your own boss may be this type – he's an energy dynamo who works himself and his people hard. He makes quick effective decisions (that may ride insensitively over subordinates' feelings) and is happiest with tight deadlines and results. When Diane questioned him that day, she made another mistake. Action-oriented bosses like Diane's take their authority very seriously. Anyone who tries to ignore that authority openly by challenging or secretly by keeping back information, does so at her peril.

Though no human being is 100 per cent one type, most people tend towards one work style and as supervisors, towards a definite management style. If like Diane and her boss, you and your boss have very different work styles, the ideal solution would be to find another job. *If today's high unemployment rate makes it impossible to change jobs, understanding your boss's personality can still make your daily work life much easier.* As soon as you do understand your supervisor's management style, you automatically become somewhat clairvoyant. You at last comprehend why he or she does 'those things' and why you react as you do. And you can foresee what kinds of behaviour on your part will please this type of supervisor; what kinds of behaviour you should avoid because they are guaranteed to displease this boss.

Besides the action-oriented and idea-oriented bosses we've already discussed, some other typical boss types are:

The 'default' boss

They court you to win you as new employees, then abandon you to sink or swim alone once you're hired. They are ill at ease with people and most comfortable with their office door shut surrounded by statistics, costs, budgets, research findings, technology. In his book *How to Manage Your Boss* (Rawson, Wade), Christopher Hegarty explains that this kind of boss can be exactly *right for you* if you have high power needs, lots of drive, desire for accomplishment, and enjoy the freedom to take charge. You only need to remember to keep this supervisor clearly and continually posted on your results. However, if you need a lot of encouragement, a personal relationship with your supervisor as well as guidance as to what you're responsible for and how to do it, you're going to have many low moments with this boss. Survival for you will depend on forcing yourself to grow independent – fast!

Feelers

They're warm and friendly. Work quarters are 'homey' with plants, personal mementos, family snapshots. They bring personal comments and interests into business conversations and will consider you unsatisfactory if you're entirely cut-and-dried and 'all business'. In working for this kind of person, logic won't be enough. You must be sensitive to their 'feelings' on the matter. Otherwise they may reject your ideas with a comment like 'Sounds good. But no. It doesn't feel right.' You discover these feelings by listening between the lines of your boss's comments. When necessary, you come right out and say, 'Here's how it might look. But I'd like to know how you feel about it.' Then pay lots of attention to satisfying those 'feelings'.

Impersonal managers

Sometimes these impersonal managers are the result of intensive business school training; sometimes it's a matter of inborn personality. One management specialist, Elton Reeves, describes this kind of supervisor as 'the greatest challenge you will have . . . she or he has mixed together human beings and the machine.' Unlike the 'feeler', the impersonal boss usually is totally disinterested in yours and her or his feelings – at least on the job. For example, explaining to this kind of boss that you need an extra-long lunch hour to buy your boyfriend a birthday present, produces no human understanding. However, this kind of boss may agree to the extra-long lunch hour if you say all your work is up to the minute and you'll make up the extra time at the end of the day if necessary. Over all, you succeed best with the impersonal boss if you concentrate on being totally practical and demonstrate the ability to plan, work, and think in ways that concentrate on business objectives.

The founder

The boss who founded the organisation you work for probably succeeded because of being highly individualistic, creative, and intuitive rather than methodical and deliberate. Unlike the impersonal boss with his charts and statistics, this 'founder' boss usually operates on a plan-as-you-go basis – and expects you to adapt. That means sudden changes in work orders, in priorities, interruptions. Because the business is this boss's 'baby', this boss is slow to delegate and will often renege or override you even if you are permitted some authority. You need the temperament to put up with this treatment as well as the willingness to accept overtime and do whatever is needed to solve today's crisis. If you like avoiding responsibility and are content to take orders, you and the founder will do well together. If you are a good administrator who enjoys following up and attending to details the founder hasn't time nor patience for, you'll do *very* well.

The survival boss

Above all this kind of supervisor wants to avoid risks. For example, the survival-supervisor sees a business meeting as a place to look good rather than as a place to make a contribution – and will expect the same behaviour from you. In his book *Managing with Style* (Amacom), management consultant Harry Golightly analyses the survivalist and concludes this type of boss 'makes decisions on the basis of what is the safest course'. If you are aggressive, ambitious and creative, you'll have to suppress these tendencies to get along with this boss. If, however, you are interested in a niche where you can come in and have a peaceful day following the routine, the survival boss and you ought to be happy together.

The leader

Golightly also describes what many feel is the 'ideal boss', the 'leader'. Though you're not likely to have a perfect 'leader' boss, you might enjoy seeing how close your supervisor comes to the model. This kind of superior has the ability to listen to and respect others and their ideas; to get to the root of problems; draw correct conclusions from data; make clear decisions; and be sensitive and considerate of people. The 'leader' values subordinates primarily for their talent and contributions and rewards accordingly.

Woman boss

Hope you rejected that heading on sight. Woman Boss is *not* a type. Yet women as well as men fall into the trap of expecting certain predictable 'woman's style' from a female supervisor. If the expected behaviour doesn't appear, they 'can't figure her out'. One research project discovered that people typically assume women managers will exhibit only two types of behaviour. Either she's going to be soft-spoken and yielding which is said to prove she 'won't rock the boat', or she's dubbed an aggressive, destructive female because she works hard and demands hard work from others. Allowing for only two kinds of behaviour is an *unrealistic* way to relate to any boss – male or female. To succeed with your woman supervisor, you have to break through the myths and expect that female bosses will exhibit the same wide range of behaviour as do male bosses.

CHAPTER 17.

Co-worker troubles and how to deal with them

When someone steals credit for your accomplishments

You may become aware that a co-worker is stealing credit for some of your achievements. Depending on your temperament, you may shrink from a confrontation and raise your blood pressure by raging silently. Or you may rush to battle.

Either reaction is a mistake. The dangers of allowing the situation to continue by ignoring it are obvious. The perils of a confrontation lie in the inevitable no-win result.

Just imagine the scene. You make your accusation. Your co-worker denies it and then begins dragging up all manner of accusations to hurl at you. In the end, the thief admits nothing. The rumours of your set-to reach your boss. Then you have to struggle with the task of convincing your superior that you are the innocent victim and that you are right.

There is an important, universal job fact involved here. When conflicts arise at work, most people devote all their energy to convincing the boss they are 'right' instead of concentrating on eliminating the conflict itself. It is the subordinate who skilfully solves controversies before they erupt that the boss values.

In most situations bosses don't really care anything at all about which employee is 'right'. A boss's interest lies in getting the work done. By becoming a party to a controversy you are slowing production. You therefore are automatically at fault in your boss's eyes, no matter how innocent you are. In fact, as an innocent victim your boss will not only consider you wrong for being part of a disruption, you will probably also be considered inept. After all, allowing yourself to be manoeuvred into your victim position is a sign of ineptness.

The only way to solve this or any potential job conflict *successfully* is by achieving your goals peacefully.

Your goal in this particular predicament involves having your boss understand that the credit belongs to you. Forget about plotting revenge. It will come to you automatically. Once your boss comprehends that you deserve the credit, your supervisor will simultaneously realise your co-worker has been lying.

To achieve your peaceful results, write a memo about the project outlining the contributions of everyone involved. Don't distract your boss by accusations. Just state the facts.

Later you can have a discussion with your boss to review the facts in your memo. The boss will almost certainly not fulfil your daydreams by storming out of her or his office and publicly castigating your opponent. But by showing the boss where the credit does lie, you've automatically made the boss sceptical about future claims by your co-worker. Without a commotion, without a confrontation, you will have achieved your goal. Most important, in your boss's eyes you will have labelled yourself as sensible and valuable.

Sexual harassment

Your supervisor, or somebody else in the organisation, makes an advance or propositions you in a way which is more or less blackmail. Can you do anything about it?

First, remember that you are not alone. A survey by the European Commission found that 7 per cent of British women had suffered from such an approach. A survey of more general sexual harassment, carried out by Thames TV and NALGO, found that more than half the women who answered complained of some harassment – 20 per cent of men complained too, of harassment by other men.

Secondly, bring the whole subject out into the open and you will often get the help and support of your co-workers (some of them may have suffered too). If you belong to a union or staff association, its officials may be able to advise and intervene if necessary. The Sex Discrimination Act doesn't cover sexual harassment, but you might win an unfair dismissal case if you were sacked because you would not give in to a proposition.

This is a subject which has only recently begun to attract attention in Britain, and it will, unfortunately, be some time before companies and individuals understand what is involved and that it is a real threat to job security and individual rights.

Coping with an unpleasant co-worker

One of the people in your department is a chronic complainer. To hear her tell it, she gets the most work, the worst assignments. She's always ready with an excuse: 'I got interrupted.' 'Nobody told me it was needed today.' 'I'm so overloaded I can't possibly do that with you now.'

If you have to work with her in order to meet your own responsibilities, you have a genuine problem.

You can help yourself best by thinking out jobs beforehand and planning your part of the work so as to have as little contact with her as possible. Also, encourage your supervisor to divide the project responsibilities and set the deadlines. When these come from your superior, you're not responsible and the woman can't bicker with you about them.

You can also help yourself by concentrating on your work goals. Instead of keeping yourself at a constant boil of exasperation by complaining to your friends and ruminating about her behaviour, finish the portion of the day's job that involves her, and go on to something more pleasant.

You might also mentally put yourself in the other woman's place and imagine how your constant annoyance with her might appear to her. Thinking of it from that angle probably won't transform the two of you into friends, but it may give you some insight into how your exasperation is fuelling her unpleasant responses. With those insights, you may find the patience to modify your impatience and perhaps win more cooperation from her.

If nothing helps and you decide you must go to your boss and ask not to be paired with her, don't attack, criticise, or downgrade her. Any time bosses hear such complaints they become suspicious of the *accuser*. Emphasise that you are interested in doing an excellent job for your boss and explain the problem as the result of two employees' different work styles, work habits, and approach to a job. Explain that your reason for asking for reassignment is based on your knowledge that you will be able to improve your production with another work partner.

When you're not accepted

When the gang at work won't accept you, just being a 'nice person' often isn't the answer. Every group is different. It has its own standards of how to dress, how to talk to one another, how to handle various situations, what attitude to take towards the employer, when humour is acceptable, and so on. Being bright, reasonably attractive, and good-hearted may actually work against you if you don't fit the group's standards. Then you have a decision to make. You may have landed in a work setting where you're instinctively not comfortable. No matter how you attempt to camouflage it, your discomfort is communicated to others, who in turn become uncomfortable with you. Or you may have landed among a tight, closed group who for private reasons of their own enjoy excluding you.

Will you be able to separate your work life from your personal life and simply do your job without any acceptance by those you work with? Most people, especially in their twenties and early thirties, find this so unpleasant a daily routine that they are served best by finding another job and leaving the scene.

The talker

Everyone enjoys a few moments of casual conversation to break up the workday. Some people seem to make a career of it. Either they lack enough work to keep them busy or they have a system for generating quantities of free time. They use that time to come around and interrupt your work while they talk and talk and talk.

Turn them off without turning them into an enemy by standing up when they arrive. Greet the talker pleasantly and mention a time limit: 'Glad to see you. Let's take 2 minutes to relax. Then I have a lot of work to do.' When the 2 minutes of pleasant conversation are up, sit down and say 'I'm really sorry but I have to get back to work now.' Then do so!

Other times you can arrange to have colleagues rescue you by breaking in to 'remind' you of an appointment or of work 'the boss wants done right away'. Since you greet the talkative co-worker pleasantly and terminate the conversation only because of your work load, soon he or she ought to find another permanent listener with more time to spare – without feeling any enmity towards you.

Deadwood dangers

You began to notice him a few weeks after you started work. He has a nice office, a good title, and not very much to do. What little he is responsible for is done poorly. His reports are late, he's vague with answers on matters he should know about. It's annoying and you're about ready to tell him so.

Better not. If you allow yourself to drift into a feud with this person, you will probably find that it is you and not he who is out of a job.

It is common for an organisation to employ a few people who have been with it for years despite their lack of competence. The very fact that men and women like this have survived without being good at their jobs is usually a sign they are being retained for some other reasons. When you discover someone like this, instead of displaying irritation you should suspect that despite the modest title and few responsibilities you are dealing with an important person in the organisation. You should go out of your way to remain on good terms with her or him.

Deadwood co-workers arrive at their powerful positions in various ways. Some started with the company during its tough beginning years and perhaps came through crucial favours. By their long association with the boss, they may also have earned a special place in the boss's affection. They may be the only ones in the organisation who remember his nickname and still have the right to use it. They may also be people whose opinions the boss is responsive to when they deliver a comment about *you*. Other co-workers become special by being related to the boss or to the boss's spouse, by being romantically involved with someone powerful with the company, or simply by having earned enough seniority to be allowed to mark time till retirement.

For your own career safety, do not be misled by the insignificant amount of work a deadwood co-worker produces. Through their seniority these people have often made themselves part of the chain who must initial requests, initial project reports, and the like. Though their initials have little active power, they can have considerable delaying clout. If you anger them, they can destroy you. They simply allow your requests, your projects, and your papers to lie and die on their desk 'till the day I have time to look at them'.

Preventing small disagreements from becoming big problems

If you're not careful, a small job disagreement can leave the other person feeling you and she or he are permanent enemies.

Marie and George are doing this as they heat up their discussion with sentences like 'That's not true,' 'I absolutely don't agree with you,' 'You're wrong.'

Marie and George could keep their verbal differences small by finding points they could agree about. They could say 'I see you're right on that matter' or 'I agree with you there.' Then they can state their own case with something like 'I think we also need to consider . . .' Anyone who really listens during a dispute can always find neutral areas to agree on: 'Yes, I certainly agree we have to have it by next Monday . . .' 'Yes, I see that your plan will get us the people we need.'

With these 'I agree' comments you maintain an atmosphere of the two of you as natural *allies* who just have to straighten out this minor matter. Also by acknowledging the various ways the other person is correct, you make it psychologically easier for that person to see and admit you also may have an acceptable idea. With negative comments such as Marie's 'I absolutely don't agree with you' you're insisting there's a wide gulf between the two of you. This can easily lead to a permanent coolness and even an ongoing active feud.

Discovering people's real personalities

If you know beforehand that someone is a jealous troublemaker, you take care not to trust him or her with personal or business secrets. If you realise someone else is timid, you know not to depend on her or him to do battle for one of your projects. Yet we've all had the shocking experience of having a co-worker we thought we knew well behave in a surprising fashion. The nice guy back-stabs or disappoints in some important way and the long-established 'cold fish' is revealed suddenly as an unusually considerate human being. By accurately understanding their true natures we could have eased our daily job lives.

Psychological research indicates that we do complicate our business lives by falling into two common psychological errors when we first meet new people:

1. We meet and relate to people within the confines of job stereotypes. We have ready-made ideas of how different types of people behave and what kinds of personalities we can expect from, say, a minister, clerk, lorry driver, secretary, banker, salesperson, teacher, business executive. At work, when we meet various of these people we *think* we are relating to them as human beings – as individuals – but in reality we commonly see only what we expect to see. We notice *only*

those traits which fit our stereotype – and we are blind to the real personality an individual is revealing to us. We 'know' that teachers are intelligent; so we don't notice that this one really isn't. We 'know' clerks have bureaucratic, boring minds and we are oblivious to the lilt and imagination in this woman's view of life.

2. We produce other co-worker troubles for ourselves by generalising from surroundings. Psychologists report that 'first impressions are lasting' is not just a cliché. It's an important fact of human behaviour. By understanding how the surroundings in which your first meeting takes place can affect you, you can guard yourself from developing impressions dangerous to you.

For example, if you meet someone for the first time in a tense setting in your boss's office, you may have an impression of his or her character as rigid and ruthless. If you're introduced to the same person over a relaxed lunch table, you might have a totally different and – if you're not careful – a permanent impression.

By meeting that person in the relaxed surrounding, you might come away with the dangerously inaccurate belief that the executive you met there is easygoing. When the axe falls on you because you misread character, you'll realise too late how deceptive impressions based on locale can be. Conversely, the person who seemed ruthless and rigid in the boss's office might be a goodhearted (and tensely anxious) co-worker who might have become one of your good friends if you hadn't used the office impression to close your mind permanently against him or her.

By learning to guard yourself against these two traps, and thereby raising your ability to size people up accurately, you avoid many co-worker hassles.

CHAPTER **18.**

Tough job situations and how to deal with them

Tough situations develop in everyone's career *no matter what kind of job it is.* When you handle the problem smoothly, it remains an unimportant, easily forgotten incident. When you panic or bungle, the problem may become a crisis that can permanently sour relationships or impede your progress to better jobs and better pay.

Here are some typical difficult situations you may face – and practical suggestions for handling them.

You don't have the equipment or authority you need

You finally rebel and tell your supervisor 'I have to have a new typewriter. I can't manage with that broken-down machine any longer. Will you get me one?'

You've just made the mistake of backing yourself against a wall.

Any time you phrase a request, as you did, so that yes or no is the *only* possible answer, you give yourself only a fifty-fifty chance of success. If the answer is 'No, you can't have what you want,' you're left looking foolish and feeling humiliated. You could have avoided that risk by saying 'I'm having trouble keeping up my share of the work because of my broken-down machine. How can I get a better one?'

With this approach, you will win something because you have given your boss a choice of many answers. Your open-ended 'How can I get a better one?' allows your boss to say the machine will be overhauled or replaced or you can borrow Mindy's while she's on vacation, or something of the sort. Even if the answer is 'Sorry, nothing I can do about it,' you haven't issued an embarrassing ultimatum. Therefore, even though you're refused you are not humiliated by having to go back and indeed manage or else launch a furious battle to save your face.

In fact, by putting the problem in a non-ultimatum fashion, you've *won* something very valuable for yourself. You've relieved yourself of the burden of worrying about your low output. You've made it clear to your supervisor that you're anxious to keep up your share of the work and that it's the company's defective equipment (or work schedule or refusal to allow you to make a decision or whatever) that is hampering you. The solution is now up to the boss and the company.

Work assignments

You were hired as an accountant. One day your supervisor tells you a typist has had an emergency operation and asks you to fill in as a typist-receptionist. Though you will be paid your usual professional accountant's pay, you feel having to spend the week typing and answering phones is not what you were trained or hired for. Can you refuse?

If the work is outside the list of your duties in your formal job description, or outside the job you were contracted to do, then you cannot be made to do it. The same applies if there is a formal union agreement which demarcates particular tasks.

So you are within your legal rights to refuse, and you may feel that in your particular company you would really jeopardise your standing by taking a lower-status job even for a week. On the other hand, if you are doing work you like for a company you like and where your prospects are good, it may be worth agreeing to help out to show how dependable you are in an emergency. But if the emergency happens more often there is something wrong with the organisation of the office, and you should point this out, firmly and tactfully. It is a waste of an accountant's skills and salary to have her employed as a typist-receptionist.

Temptation

You desperately want or need to take a day off but you don't want to use your personal leave for it. Is it safe to invent some plausible company-paid excuse for the absence?

Better not. When you offer your excuse it will be entered on the record and you will be guilty of a serious lie. If it were discovered, you might even be sacked and you would certainly qualify for a written warning to be placed on your file. And the organisation would be unlikely to trust you in the future.

Your boss wants you to spy

People in your organisation are exploring the possibility of joining a union. Your boss wants you to report what's discussed at pro-union meetings and who attends.

The right to belong to a trade union, and not to suffer discrimination as a result, is a very strongly guarded one in Britain. Be a friend to your boss by reminding him of the dangers of such an approach – from a major press scandal to legal actions by staff members who think they have been victimised for their union activities.

Personal problems

Sometimes job crises can result not from what you say but from your decision to say nothing. The situation of an unfortunate woman, Meryll Sean, is typical. Meryll's widower father was battling cancer. By day Meryll worked at her job. Evenings, mornings, and weekends she tended her father as he suffered the physical and emotional effects of the disease and chemotherapy. Like many people, Meryll believed that carrying on one's work responsibilities without 'bothering' people with your personal troubles is the grown-up way to behave. She carefully refrained from discussing her 24-hour-a-day, seven-day-a-week nightmare with her colleagues.

Though she thought she behaved normally at work, she wasn't completely herself. Sometimes there were lapses in her job performance and she was sometimes absent-minded or short with people. Her new habit of rushing home after work made people think she had become very unfriendly. Her boss and co-workers were becoming seriously annoyed with her when someone accidentally discovered the real situation and spread the word.

It's true you're inviting job trouble if you say very much about some types of private anxieties such as martial or romantic difficulties or embarrassing legal or monetary dilemmas. Workplace gossip about them can undermine your total job position. Yes, for practical reasons you have to mention it if you're getting a divorce. You can't have people you work with erroneously believing you're married when you're not. To do that turns all the mechanics of your daily small talk and social relationships into a deception. But the details of why are no one's business. Yet when there is a serious illness in the family or other such trouble, it's dangerous and foolish to say too little. You can't overdo it and expect colleagues to carry your work load or absorb long daily tales of your troubles. Telling them about it in moderate amounts means they'll understand and probably make allowances for your occasional lapses. By informing them of the situation you avoid the risk of ending up with *two* monumental problems: trouble at home and alienated colleagues at work.

Someone with less responsibility is earning more than you

You've just found out. Not only does the other person have less responsibility, she hasn't been working for the organisation as long as you have. Yet she earns more.

What do you do?

Professional labour mediator Edward Levin points out that the ideal solution in this and any tough job situation enables *both* you and your boss to feel you've won. Getting your increase and leaving your boss with the feeling of having been caught being unfair to you, he says, is not really winning.

Mr Levin suggests you quietly tell your boss that you're troubled because you've learned of this inequity in salary between you and the other employee. But don't whine or accuse; that kind of behaviour boomerangs against you because it intensifies the guilt your boss probably already feels. If you intensify this guilt, you make your boss angry – with you! It's not logical or fair, but it's human nature. Instead, try to soothe the boss's defensive feelings. Acknowledge that you understand the situation. Maybe the new employee had unusual credentials or the organisation desperately needed someone for that job.

Whatever the reason, you're saying you understand why the boss was forced to offer that amount to hire the person. But now since you're also contributing so much – calmly list your responsibilities, successes, and plans for future projects – you'd like your salary adjusted to what you're worth. Be sure to name the sum that seems just. Mr Levin explains that this attitude should produce the feeling you've both won. You can obtain the money you deserve and your boss can feel the episode caused you to take stock and plan ahead to sharpen your job efforts.

If however, your boss refuses to adjust your salary or deal with the situation, then you have to ask yourself *new* basic questions: 'Why is my boss so uninterested in treating me fairly? Is it a sign that he or she doesn't really think I'm a valuable employee? Should I start looking elsewhere for another job?'

Your secret career interests

For a long time now you've been interested in learning a high-paying manual skill like that of electrician. Everyone you've confided in warns you you're not facing reality. They insist you'll be so unhappy in the rough work conditions and the male reactions to your 'invading' their jobs that the good pay won't be worth it.

Chances are you'll be very happy if you ignore the well-intentioned advice and follow your inclinations. A Yale psychologist's study of women who entered 'male' occupations (and men who entered 'female' occupations such as clerical work) revealed that these people are likely to be happier than they would have been if they forced themselves to continue with jobs traditionally associated with their sex. The researcher believes that the non-traditional women job-holders felt so pleased with their own life because they had gravitated to a career that allowed them to use their inborn talents. Surprisingly, the extra pressure to prove themselves in their breakthrough jobs seemed also to add to the women's pleasure in their work.

When you're the supervisor

Someone who works for you is bright and capable but not interested in her work. She rushes through everything rather than thinking about each project she works on. If possible, you'd rather motivate her to do better than replace her with someone new who has to be trained.

Supervisors often discover that poor work is the result of a poor understanding of what is expected. Have you ever really discussed the requirements of the job with her? Or have you merely criticised flaws in her work? She may know you are dissatisfied but may not have a clear understanding of how exactly you would like things done or the reasons why it is important to do it that way.

A private talk may solve the problem. Concentrate on the positive: the things she should be doing. Be specific about the job requirements, output, standards you want her to reach. And don't trap yourself into talking about her personality or attitude. This is not a personal problem between you two. It is a job situation and the problem is one of adjusting her performance.

Motivating people who work for you is a complex task.

Scores of books have been written on the subject. Anyone who becomes a manager will make her own on-the-job life easier by studying a few of them. One of the best – readable and practical – is *Understanding People at Work* by Thomas L. Quick, published by Executive Enterprises Publications, New York.

You've been fired

This is the ultimate unpleasant job situation. How do you explain it in a curriculum vitae or during a job interview?

Being fired ceases to be a stigma if you indicate you left your job for a reason that had nothing to do with your job performance. Some acceptable reasons for having left a position include: (1) a new boss wanted to build her or his own team or arrived with her or his own team; (2) cutbacks due to business slowdown; and (3) department mergers that created extra employees. Personality conflicts with your old boss can *sometimes* be an acceptable explanation – but only when he or she is widely known in your town or industry as a tyrant, erratic, or something similar. If the boss has no such reputation, avoid the personality conflict reason lest the prospective employer wonder whether you're the one who is difficult to get along with.

Night safety

This tough situation could cost you physical harm because you often have to work late in a nearly deserted building. There are night watchmen, but what else can you do to add to your safety and make yourself feel less anxious?

Whenever possible, eliminate the problem by taking work home or arriving earlier the following morning. When you must stay, some simple safety rules are:

1. Work *only* where others are in the room or a nearby area. If necessary, move your work to where the others are.

2. Keep a phone close by and memorise the security guards' phone numbers.

3. Get yourself a whistle and keep it accessible.

4. In a lift stand close to the button panel. In case of attack or threat, press the alarm button and as many other floor buttons as possible to stop the elevator at the next floor. But don't press the Stop button; that will trap you between floors with your attacker.

CHAPTER 19.

When is loyalty to your job a mistake?

Do any of the following describe you?

1. Every office has a lot of nuisance jobs. Because I am always willing to do them when they turn up, I am impressing my boss with my value as a promotable employee.

2. I would like to do my job so well that my boss will think of me as indispensable.

3. People who work with me know that when they're over-loaded they can always count on me to help them for the sake of the department.

4. Though I'll do the extra odds and ends when I'm asked to, I don't go out of my way to look for them.

5. If I heard about an opening in another department that was a better job possibility for me, I'd go straight to that department head or personnel and let them know I'm interested.

6. A few years ago the company I work for took a chance on me and gave me a supervisory position at a good salary. There's no place else I can move up. But I feel it would be

flighty and ungrateful to go elsewhere. I think the best thing is to wait patiently. Maybe something will open up here.

Now find out how your ideas about job loyalty are affecting your career opportunities.

What you owe others on a job situation versus what you owe yourself

You do owe your boss and the company your full loyalty. But unless you understand the difference between sensible, businesslike loyalty and misplaced, overdone loyalty, you can lock yourself into a career dead end.

Barbara Pontier, who has worked in a corporate office for four years, recently became aware that she is facing this dead-end problem. She doesn't quite understand how it happened to her. Her boss relies on her, frequently praises her, has even told her he 'couldn't do without her'. She's popular with her co-workers and they know she can always be depended upon to help them with their work. She's received modest rises but basically she's doing the same work now that she did three years ago. She's concerned by the fact that a few of her co-workers have moved on to better jobs in other departments. The last time it happened she asked her boss about it. He reminded her of how essential she is to everyone in the department and arranged another small rise for her. She says, 'I don't quite understand whether I'm better off going along this way . . . or even exactly what is going on. What should I be doing?'

Barbara is misinterpreting loyalty. In her eagerness to show her boss how loyal and conscientious she is, she has tagged herself as indispensable and turned herself into the department drudge.

Under ordinary circumstances, the extra nuisance jobs would be spread around so everyone would have to share them graciously. But when someone like Barbara comes along and accepts the drudgery assignments eagerly, human nature takes control and she is exploited. Sometimes bosses may deliberately play on such loyalty; other bosses (and co-workers too) take advantage of overdone loyalty without realising what's happening.

The scenario may go like this: Co-worker to boss: 'Oh, you need this by four o'clock? I won't be able to get all this done by then. Can I ask Barbara to help me?' Boss: 'Sure. Get Barbara to help.' Or, when the boss has to assign some undesirable task, the thought may be 'Why give this to Karen or George or Bill or Linda, who might have to be "sold" on going it? I'll give it to Barbara. No matter what she's asked to do, she's so agreeable.'

The result of all this is that Barbara is so loaded down with all the routine 'garbage' that she never has a chance to take on any of the newer projects that come through the department. Her co-workers get those; they have the time. Sometimes those new, broadening responsibilities give her co-workers the credentials to move to a better job in the company or to leave for a better job elsewhere.

By allowing her conscientiousness to be channelled into meaningless, drudgery tasks, Barbara shuts herself away from promotion in a *second* way. Whenever the question of transferring someone to a better position arises, every boss inevitably considers two questions: 'Who can do the new job?' and 'Whom can I afford to lose?' When someone else is about equal in competence to Barbara, the boss will usually steer the other person into the new position.

By making herself so indispensable Barbara has forced her supervisor to decide that she couldn't afford to lose Barbara. It doesn't matter whether the boss's decision is made on a coldly self-serving level or on an innocent, subconscious level. The result for Barbara is the same. She stays at her present job and someone else moves up.

By applying the same loyalty and conscientiousness in a slightly different way, Barbara Pontier could be of value to her boss, her company, and to herself. She should graciously do *her* share of the drudgery, her share of helping co-workers through emergencies, but she should reserve her active enthusiasm only for growth assignments. Loyalty and conscientiousness would be evident to her superior when she says 'If something new comes in, I'd like to take a crack at it.' Better yet, she can anticipate new assignments. That's where she should volunteer 'Do you need someone to organise the presentation for the new project? I'd be willing to try it.' Or 'Do you need someone to help you work out the budget allocations? I can stay late all this week.' In doing this she increases her 'use potential' for the company as well as for herself.

Saving yourself from your predicament

Someone like Barbara Pontier who has built the wrong image can extricate herself by altering her behaviour. She can list her job accomplishments and what she'd like to do, make an appointment with her boss, and say something like 'It doesn't seem like it but do you know I've been here nearly four years? When I started, I was responsible for only a small area. Now I do so much more. I've learned a lot with you. And now I believe I'm ready to go on to such-and-such other kinds of department jobs. That would give other people experience in some of the things I've been doing.' After discussing what she's been responsible for and what she's interested in taking on, she leaves the lists with her boss.

The next time the boss automatically hands her a drudge task, she can remind her or him that she'd rather do the other kinds of assignments. 'It's only fair for someone else to have a chance for these jobs I've been carrying.' The boss has a high regard for her; he sees her as indispensable and is certainly not going to turn on her if she acts this way. Instead, any sensible boss is quickly going to realise that he/she should start giving Barbara some of the better assignments and spread the junk around. Or she'll leave. As she ceases to do the 'garbage', Barbara will cease to be so indispensable that she stands in the way of her own promotion.

With her co-workers Barbara can produce a fairer workload distribution by reversing her usual reaction. When they try shovelling some of their work at her, she can pleasantly explain that she's overloaded: 'Please, would you help me with some of mine for today?' It won't take long.

PART V

GETTING AHEAD

CHAPTER 20.

Getting ahead within your company

Unless you know how to handle the situation, private agreements among company executives can keep you from a better position and a higher salary. 'Don't steal my people and I won't steal yours' is a common understanding among executives. Under these conditions how do you get yourself an interdepartmental promotion?

Secretly applying for a better job in another department is not the answer. Though you initiate the application, the other boss will not be free of the 'don't-steal' taboo. Your solution lies in doing just the opposite. When you hear of a position that interests you, you handle it by going *first* to your boss. 'There's a position open in Department X that would be an advance for me. I feel I could do the work. I'd like to apply. Please, would you recommend me?'

With this approach, *you win either way*. If your boss tries to talk you out of it – without offering you concrete expectations of advancement within your current department – then you know it's time to start job-hunting. Continued patience here means a dead end.

If your boss reacts positively and promises to recommend you, you've eliminated the private-agreement barrier. After your boss recommends you the other supervisor will no longer be stealing and will feel free to consider you.

But what about the situation where twice your boss has told you he or she would take care of everything yet you didn't get the promotion-transfer either time? How can you find out if the boss really did recommend you?

In a small company go to the other supervisor and ask 'Could you tell me what qualifications I lacked for that job so I can be better prepared next time?' Again, either way, you win. Either the supervisor explains what additional credentials you need or the supervisor looks surprised and says 'I didn't know you were interested in the job.' And there's your warning against ever again relying on your boss's promises.

In a larger company, besides obtaining your boss's recommendation, you will probably have to apply at personnel. Later, when you are interviewed, you can learn the truth about your boss's promises. Personality questions, pleasantries about the company, general conversation all mean your boss has not followed through and the other supervisor still thinks you're 'off limits'. Serious interest by the other boss would be revealed by discussion of what work you've done, your job training, specifications of the new work, and similar matters.

A third situation often exists. Beyond the private executive understandings, in some companies there is a general policy under which managers work together to keep interdepartmental movement and subsequent upheaval to a minimum. In these organisations your boss and the other supervisors may cooperate with smooth explanations for why you weren't chosen. Yet you may notice that those who fill the positions usually seem to be hired from outside. Look around. Check with friends in other departments. If it is rare for anyone to move up from department to department, you have your answer.

Always an assistant, never a boss

When her second boss in four years was promoted to a better job, one young woman became impatient. She was fortunate in having an uncle with twenty-five years' experience as a senior corporate executive. He advised her 'Tell them you've already taught the ropes to two people for that supervisor's job and you're still the assistant. You have four years' experience in this kind of work and you know how the company operates. In the intervals between bosses, you've done the work. Now you'd like to have the job. Remind them they wouldn't ask you to "show" these new people if they were unsure of your ability to make the decisions and do the work involved.'

The situation of a secretary or assistant who keeps breaking in managers who then move on while she stands still is common. Today, with government pressure on companies to promote women, your chances of escaping the always-the-assistant-but-never-the-boss trap are excellent.

Unless you *actively* seek the job, though, you may never get it. The fact that you are a very competent assistant produces in management the powerful desire to leave you exactly where you are. As they see it, if they move you up, they have to worry about you proving yourself as well as whether your replacement will succeed. They will have two problems. If they just replace the supervisor, they have only one problem, with that one softened by the presence of a first-rate assistant.

When, however, you ask for the supervisor's job as the corporate executive suggested, you force the top people to see it from your viewpoint. If they refuse with a 'we need you where you are', your logical response should be 'Do you mean then I'll never move ahead?'

They're not going to reply 'Yes, you're stuck.' They don't want to start you thinking about leaving. If they can, they may try to tempt you to stay where you are with a salary increase. Or having been forced to rethink the situation, the decision may come from above. 'All right. We'll give you a chance.'

Now be prepared for another common problem. Suppress the impulse to exclaim 'Oh, wonderful. Thank you.' Instead, *immediately* settle the title and money questions. Immediately! Talk specifically! Don't say 'Will I get the usual salary that goes with the job?' Say 'That means then I will be the new supervisor of ____ at the usual £_____ salary the last two people started at?' (If you're not sure, guess higher. The final agreement will be closer to the truth.)

Often the reaction to your question will be 'Oh, no. This is just a trial. You have to prove you can handle it. If in six months . . .'

When that happens, the corporate executive told his niece, you can say 'If I'm going to do the work, then I should have the title, salary, and office that go with it. The people I've helped learn the ins and outs of this job had the salary, title, and office when they were on trial. You hire them from outside when you don't know them and give them everything the job calls for. You don't know whether they will be successful. You gamble on them.

'Me, you know! You call on me to show new supervisors what the job requires. Therefore my chances of success are equal to or better than those people. If they have the title, salary, and office *during* the trial period, I should too. Besides, I'm extra-valuable. I not only know the supervisor's job, I know how to train my replacement.'

The bottom line

If your boss and your company cannot or will not allow you to move to better jobs and higher salaries as your abilities expand, then it's time for you to go promotion-hunting elsewhere!

CHAPTER 21.

Would they <u>really</u> promote a woman to the job you want?

Six dependable signs

Though the scrap of newspaper is almost a year old and beginning to yellow, Betty still keeps the help-wanted ad that lured her into her present administrative assistant job: 'Xcellent oppty. Very promotable.' Yet Betty is beginning to wonder. She's received a rise, but nobody's even hinted at a promotion.

Karla began as a management trainee. Yesterday she was offered a transfer to sales administrator with a pay increase. Is it really a step up? Will it lead to bigger and better jobs? She has to let them know by Monday.

Florence has decided to chuck her personnel-interviewer work. She feels it doesn't serve her long-range ambitions. 'Some day,' says Florence, 'I'd like to be in a big corner office with a secretary and staff of my own. But I'm puzzled. Every Sunday I see dozens of ads offering all kinds of possibilities in sales, management, personnel advertising. I have the education and skills to apply for a number of the ads and many are in my salary range. How do I decide which ads to pursue? How do I know which represent the best promotion potential?'

In 1973, the British job market changed. That year, the Sex Discrimination Act was passed, and the business community realised it could no longer ignore women's job rights. Companies realised that they had better promote women *or at least look as if* they are interested in promoting women.

Since then every ambitious woman has faced the problem of separating the companies that are sincere about letting them rise as far as their talents will take them from the companies that do the legal minimum. *In other words, you have to be able to distinguish between companies that would really promote you to important positions from those that are kidding you along to keep the government away from their doors. How do you tell the difference?*

There are six dependable signs you can use to select the right jobs within the right companies. They were developed by the international research firm Ernest Dichter Associates International, Ltd, headed by 'The Father of Motivational Research,' Dr Ernest Dichter. These signs were not derived from short-term investigations. They are insights developed by the Dichter organisation as it worked intimately over the years with hundreds of major companies on all manner of organisational and motivational problems.

David Nierenberg, former executive director of the Dichter research organisation, was responsible for isolating and analysing the telltale six. To get the facts we arranged a lengthy interview with him. Mr Nierenberg, who now heads his own manpower evaluation and development company in White Plains, New York, is also an adjunct professor of management development and the author of a column about corporate problems that appears in a group of the Gannett newspapers.

Visible jobs or hidden jobs?

Do most executive women in your company hold visible jobs where the public (and the law) can see them going about their duties? Or are women moving into *both* visible and hidden responsibilities? If the women with titles are exclusively in visible jobs like consumer relations, public relations, community relations, customer relations, and credit relations rather than in the more basic work of the corporation, it probably indicates *surface* conformity.

This doesn't mean you should automatically refuse visible positions or abandon a visible-oriented company. The visible job of director of public relations or assistant to the director of consumer relations might be exactly what you're after or they might be precisely the stepping stones to your personal career goals. Surveying your company's visible-hidden mix is simply a tool for you to use in judging its basic attitude.

Path or rut?

Though she couldn't put it into words, Karla hesitated about her new job offer because she sensed that the sales-administrator position might be a rut rather than a path. The same job title can mean different things in different companies. Before her Monday deadline, Karla has to investigate her organisation's interpretation.

If Karla discovers she cannot see two or three promotion positions beyond the job offered her, there is no path. Some organisations will say 'We really want you to have a total understanding of our business and though you don't see any further progress in this job, we intend to move you to another area to give you broader exposure.'

'Don't believe it!' warns Nierenberg. A change in management or a change in a key manager and you are forgotten. If you are not allowed to rely on your own performance to progress, you have been shunted into a job rut. When you are forced to depend on someone higher up to open a career path for you, your employer is misleading you and your chances for promotion are doubtful.

Is the work *varied or repetitive?* This is another easy way to tell a path from a rut. For instance, if you have a report-writing job that gives you a chance for both input and a variety of reports, you're probably on a path. But a recording job that allows only repetitive input is probably a rut.

Whether the duties of your job are *segregated into a cul-de-sac or integrated into the organisation as a whole* can also be a tipoff. If you don't have exposure and integration into other areas at least on a communication basis, you don't know what's happening within the company and you're in a segregated rut. Most clerical work is segregated. However, here again you have to judge each job by its character. Doing clerical assignments for the sales manager of a sales-oriented company might give you the opportunity to learn enough about the basic business of the company to win promotion into sales and the organisation's main power line.

Musical slots

Is it an advance or just a version of the old musical chairs game where you keep changing places but one place is very like the others? This also troubled Karla. She wondered whether the sales-administrator work represented a true advance or only duplication of her present status under the guise of a new assignment. A genuine advance would probably give Karla – and you – more authority, more responsibility, more pay, and perhaps more subordinates.

Yet not all 'musical slots' are worthless to you. Some may have ultimate promotion value by giving you exposure to new skills and to new valuable executive and customer contacts that slide you closer to the real promotion line.

After you've examined any individual job in terms of your personal goals, you can use the 'musical slots' test again to look over the kinds of promotions most women in your company receive. If most are going round and round with new titles but no significant upward movement, you've learned something about the company's true plans.

Staff and line

This is one of the most important distinctions in the job world. *More than anything else it often determines who reaches the highest echelons of a company and who doesn't.* Yet most women never hear a word about it. Once Florence understands the difference between line jobs and staff jobs, she will find it vastly easier to choose among the Sunday ads.

Line jobs are action jobs, as we noted in Chapter 1, pages 18–19. A line position is directly involved in or responsible for the production or sale of a company's product or service. Staff jobs are support jobs. The staff positions support line with information, research, advice, or assistance. Some staff jobs would be data processing, public relations, market planning, personnel, industrial relations, purchasing, accounting, and engineering.

However, if the company itself is a public relations firm or accounting firm or engineering firm, then in those companies the *product* is public relations work, or accounting work, or engineering designs. And in those companies public relations *or* accounting *or* engineering would be line.

All you have to do is stop and think what the main business of your company is. Anyone directly involved in producing or selling that product is in a line position and is on the fast track.

It is far easier to rise fast and high in line work than in staff. That is because line work is quantitative and can be measured and judged while staff work is amorphous and is hard to judge.

For instance, suppose you're in staff research. How can you distinguish yourself? You gather information and present it. There's no way for others to evaluate fully what's involved, to determine whether you are an excellent researcher compared to someone else who is good but not excellent.

In line work it's easy to evaluate performance. If the sales goal is £5,000 a week and you or your sales people are bringing in £6,000, you're tremendous. You get reward and recognition. If you're bringing in £4,500 you get warned. Everyone can judge exactly how you're doing. 'Consequently,' says Nierenberg, 'the ladder to the top is more easily blocked in the staff area. It's line that "closes the deal," that turns out the right product at the right price. We're talking about the battle ribbons. Everyone likes to promote a winner. Look what Mary or John did! They beat the quota!'

How about your company? Even if you prefer staff work, the presence of a significant number of women in the fast-track line jobs tells you the company is truly interested in promoting women. When this is true about line, it's logical for you to assume that promotions available within your staff area will also be open to women.

Training, yes or no?

Betty would be less anxious about her promotion chances if she went back and reread other portions of the help-wanted ad she's saved. 'Training programme and in-house development' were also tucked into it. A company that advertises training programmes for women in entry positions (or makes them available through company policy once you're hired) is demonstrating sincerity about promoting women. Betty is taking evening courses at her company's expense and just last week her supervisor suggested she might be interested in an in-house seminar on the company's total management philosophy.

When her supervisor mentioned the philosophy seminar, Betty was peeved. Of course she said yes. But the girl in the next office, whose job is the same as Betty's, has been asked to join what Betty describes as 'a great, specific course about the company's new bookkeeping methods instead of the vague seminar about philosophy they dropped me into.'

Betty's reaction is wrong. Her company is clearly more interested in Betty as executive material than they are in the woman in the next office. But until Betty and other women understand the promotional implications of different kinds of company training programmes they cannot accurately interpret their companies' promotion intentions.

Job skills or broad company skills

There are three possible attitudes a company can take about increasing your job skills. Starting from the bottom up:

1. No training. Do your job, we'll pay you, and be happy about it!

2. We're going to give you some technical skills that relate to your job. Then when a spot opens up, maybe we'll move you into it.

3. We're going to educate you about (a) the whole company, (b) total management philosophy, (c) management skills. You're promotable.

The new bookkeeping skills offered to Betty's neighbour represent Type 2 training, which can lift her one or two notches in the company. The Type 3 management philosophy Betty has a chance for can lead to the top. Valuable specific Type 3 training includes supervision, management, finance, sales, production processes, communication, leadership, decision-making, time organisation, motivation, and the like.

The job you personally are after may involve new techniques rather than broad company skills. But whether or not your company is offering Type 3 to *some* women remains a sure sign of the company's overall intentions towards the women who work for it.

Feedback

Betty could also have saved herself anxiety if she had understood the meaning of job feedback. She's had two performance reviews, both favourable. At the time she accepted the job she was informed of the review procedures. She inwardly groaned but nevertheless decided to join the company. The existence of these review feedback procedures was something Betty should have welcomed, not resented.

In fact, it's the other way around. If personnel people look astonished when you ask about performance reviews and 'We don't see any need for them,' *then* you have something to worry about. The fact that nobody is actively interested in how you're doing can be a signal that they don't see the job as the path you thought it was.

David Nierenberg sums up: 'The absence of strong interest in performance feedback is not a fatal sign. It is one of the six indicators that you use for your overview. This is not a perfect world. You're probably not going to find any company that scores 100 on all six signs.

'At a certain stage you have to decide on the basis of the criteria "They're a company that shows positive interest in promoting women. I can probably make it with them." The important point is to learn to explore situations accurately and start moving.'

QUIZ

What are your promotion chances? Rate your company and your job

1. Who holds the visible executive positions in your company?
   a. Males.
   b. Females.
   c. Pretty equally divided.

2. How many positions beyond your current position are likely to be yours sometime within the near future?
   a. None clearly yours. You're told 'We'll have a place for you.'
   b. The two next levels up or same level in another larger division.
   c. Unlimited. You're told 'You'll be qualified for quite a few, which we can discuss at a later date.'

3. How much creativity and personal input do you have in your position?
   a. None – 'Just do what's laid out.'
   b. A bit.
   c. Can do as you see fit – 'You can make this job what you want it to be.'

4. How difficult will it be for you and for others to measure your performance and contributions to the company?
   a. Very difficult to measure.
   b. Specific performance goals established.
   c. I don't really know.

5. Will the training offered to you
   a. Involve managerial concepts?
   b. Be very skill-oriented?
   c. Represent a mixture of both?

6. Is there a training programme available to you permitting your selection of courses?
   a. Yes.
   b. No.
   c. I never checked into the matter.

143

SCORING FOR QUIZ

3 POINTS	1 POINT	NO POINTS
1. C	B	A
2. B	C*	A
3. C**	B	A
4. B	C	A
5. A	C	B
6. A	C	B

* Qualified: Although we give only one point for C, there may be quite an opportunity here. But it requires more specific pinning down. You should try to get them to talk with you and focus on some specific areas, some specific career paths.

** C requires a warning relating to the performance evaluation. It's an opportunity *provided* you'll have predetermined objectives and measurable criteria set forth.

What your score means

18–12   The commitment by your company is sincere and represents a good opportunity for you.

11–6   The outcome is in doubt. Better get some more information and clarify where you'll be headed in the long run.

5–0   Watch out! There's only surface commitment to equality.

CHAPTER 22

Understanding what your boss thinks of you

If yours is one of the many companies that uses evaluation forms to rate employee performance, you never have to guess what your boss thinks of you. It's all there checked out for you – often with comments – in the little boxes of your company's evaluation form. Your final score will probably be influential in determining whether you keep your job and whether you receive pay increases and promotions.

How the boss rates you

Until recently ratings were used only for non-union factory workers. Nowadays white-collar workers and even some professionals are evaluated, usually once a year.

What your boss demands obviously depends on your occupation. Someone in personnel work may have to earn high marks in human relations while for a computer operator social skills might be of little importance. For a salesperson there may be questions about 'Is she in a rut for customer presentations?' 'Keeps comfortably ahead of call schedule?' All employees are usually judged for such characteristics as accuracy, friendliness, drive, personal appearance, dependability, quantity of work, courtesy, and stability.

The idea of rating professionals is still new, even experimental. A personnel manager reports that 'All of a sudden they're counting how many people I interview, how many of them stay on and for how long, what their production is after they're here for a while, and so on.' One legal firm even tried to determine what kinds of litigation their lawyers were most skilled at by analysing the lawyers' speed in completing various cases. Supervisors and executives may be judged on qualities such as motivating subordinates with questions such as 'Does the supervisor praise employees when they do a good job?' 'Does she play favourites?'

Below is a section of a typical employee rating form. In addition to the boxes for check marks this form allows space for the boss's remarks. You are always much better off if your company requires check-plus-comment. Having to justify the check-placement with a sentence or two of evidence forces your supervisor to think through how she or he is rating you. For example, your boss can't just quickly tick off a poor rating for you on dependability and then move on. He or she is going to have to comment, giving examples of your work that justify the low rating. Being forced to stop and consider the comment often helps the boss realise that only one or two isolated instances of poor dependability performance were involved; that usually you are dependable. That, in turn, often leads the boss to upgrade the score you receive for the job characteristic.

The check-and-comment method is the type of evaluation your boss is most likely to use for you; in a recent major survey 78 per cent of the responding companies reported they use this evaluation method.

In these forms each rating has different point values, depending on the job and the company. For example, 'satisfactory' for 'Cooperation' in the form above might be worth four points for one job and only two for another. Your total score is added up and may be placed on a graph showing your relative competence compared with your co-workers in similar jobs. If your total for all the questions is 85, you'll be up there on the graph above your co-workers who scored 79 and 83 but below your department whizkid who rated 91.

ACCURACY: ability to perform assigned work correctly and as required.

POOR	FAIR	SATISFACTORY	VERY SATISFACTORY	OUTSTANDING
☐ makes frequent errors.	☐ often repeats errors; careless.	☐ makes average number of mistakes, usually accurate.	☐ makes few mistakes, requires little supervision.	☐ rarely makes mistakes with very little supervision.

Remarks:

ALERTNESS: ability to grasp instructions quickly, to adjust to changes, to recognise new situations.

POOR	FAIR	SATISFACTORY	VERY SATISFACTORY	OUTSTANDING
☐ slow to 'catch on' or to respond.	☐ requires more than average instruction, direction, explanation.	☐ demonstrates average ability with some explanation and direction.	☐ usually quick to understand with little explanation.	☐ demonstrates exceptional aptitude.

Remarks:

COOPERATION: ability to work harmoniously with different people, groups, and supervisors.

POOR	FAIR	SATISFACTORY	VERY SATISFACTORY	OUTSTANDING
☐ does not work well with others; antagonistic.	☐ occasional difficulty in working with others; tactless.	☐ works well with others when requested to do so, agreeable.	☐ takes initiative in working with others; always willing to help.	☐ sought out by others to work with; inspires co-workers.

Remarks:

DEPENDABILITY: ability to complete assignments and perform tasks with a minimum of supervision.

POOR	FAIR	SATISFACTORY	VERY SATISFACTORY	OUTSTANDING
☐ requires close supervision, is unreliable.	☐ requires some 'follow-up' to ensure desired performance.	☐ usually completes assigned tasks with reasonable promptness.	☐ requires little supervision, can be relied upon.	☐ requires practically no supervision to complete assignment.

Remarks:

An interesting new system that is gaining acceptance requires your boss to keep written records of how you react to problem situations. You may be rated as: did/did not see problem; recognised/overlooked cause of problem; recognised/failed to see a special situation. The boss's written comment for one week for someone who wasn't performing well might be 'Failed to see special situation. Special delivery letter on important matter arrived at about same time as regular mail. Instead of bringing it to my attention, she placed it in my in-tray with routine correspondence.'

What you can do about it

After your supervisor completes the appraisal, you'll probably be treated to what personnel departments sometimes term the 'tell and sell' approach. You're shown your scores. Your boss explains the reasons for the ratings and discusses how you can improve your performance and then may ask for your reactions. Most of the time (89 per cent in a recent survey) you have an opportunity to sign the report. Printed on the form is usually a statement indicating that your signature doesn't necessarily mean you agree with your boss's judgments. Allowing you to sign is a safeguard companies provide for employees to ensure you've been permitted to see the report before it is placed in your file.

If you really feel you've been misjudged, you have various recourses. A minority of companies have space near your signature where you can comment on your supervisor's appraisal. If there is no space, you can write a memo explaining your views and have it attached to the form. Probably most effective is a calm discussion with your supervisor wherein you try to have the ratings altered by asking for examples of why you've received the poor rating. If you remember one or two episodes where you failed, bring them up and ask if perhaps these few 'flops' have overshadowed the numerous times (mention some specifically) when you have usually succeeded. Many fair-minded bosses – when you do it pleasantly – will realise that perhaps a few atypical errors you made did over-influence the rating you received.

Overall, your ratings can be an important aid to you. By controlling your natural urge to argue about every critical comment, you will learn how you can strengthen your job performance. After all, *sometimes* your boss is right!

By listening attentively to what your boss *emphasises* you will also gain an insight into which parts of your job your boss considers most important. One young stockbroker listened and realised that her constantly appearing busy was very important to her boss and all the executives in the organisation. For these bosses, production was not sufficient. You had to *look* actively involved. In another case an elementary-school teacher listened and realised that neat classroom bulletin boards and window shades evenly drawn were more important to her principal than imaginative lessons that kept the children eager to learn. The teacher didn't abandon her interesting lessons, but she did accept the fact she'd have to devote more time to 'nonsense' like window shades and tacks for bulletin boards.

Listening carefully to the rating discussion can also permit you to foresee your own future in the organisation. Do they seem to see you as someone with potential? Fine, concentrate on moving ahead within the organisation. Are your appraisals usually mediocre? You now know that for career progress you must make plans to seek a job elsewhere.

If your ratings are low

No rating or evaluation method is completely accurate. The process involves a human being rating other human beings. Therefore, as your boss rates you, there are endless possibilities for human misjudgments, prejudices, office politics, and honest differences of opinion. As Kenneth S. Teel, professor of Human Resources Management at California State University and a specialist in employee performance appraisal puts it, 'A score say of 88 out of a possible 100 implies an ability for precise measurement that does not exist.' He explains that where someone scores 82 and another person rates 88, the difference between the two is probably meaningless and could easily be reversed if the rating were done by another supervisor. So if your rating is unsatisfactory to you and you're sure your boss is mistaken, don't let it depress you or destroy your confidence in yourself. Find another job and let another boss discover how competent you really are.

CHAPTER 23.

How to ask for
a rise – and get it

Getting a rise involves two things: being worth a rise and getting your superiors to understand exactly how valuable you are to them. When you are worth a rise and your superiors clearly understand your value, they will feel justified in giving you the increase. As your employers will probably see it, it's pleasanter *for them* than losing you and struggling to find a competent replacement who may have to be paid as much as or more than you're asking.

It's true there are times when you won't receive an increase even though your boss is aware of your worth. You may be refused when: (1) your company's financial condition is poor; (2) you are at the top of the salary range for that job; (3) your superior insists she appreciates you but 'they' won't approve anything but a token amount.

It doesn't matter whether these excuses are true or not. Each informs you that you've reached a dead end with this company. If you are to progress, you'll have to search for a different job – so your request was fruitful after all. Through it you've saved yourself from wasting months or years while you vainly hoped and waited.

What exactly do you do?

You make an appointment with your boss and discuss the reasons you think entitle you to more money. You can use our six basic suggestions below as a point-by-point outline for your discussion. *You don't have to be able to document each of the six points.* Your facts may fit only one or two of the categories. Yet they may be sufficient to indicate that the company will profit by agreeing to a suitable increase.

At the end of your talk leave your supervisor with a memo that restates all your reasons. Nobody can remember everything others say in a discussion. Listening experts have found that immediately after a conversation the average person recalls only 50 per cent of what is said. A day later people recall less than 25 per cent. Talking with your superior has set the mood. Later your boss can study your memo and also use it as a powerful aid with anyone else concerned in the final decision.

How to let them know you're worth it

1. List ways your responsibilities have expanded since your last salary adjustment. Since your employers are receiving more from you, it should make good sense to them to compensate you better.

2. List any ways that you have increased your boss's value to her or his superior and to the company. If you've taken over tasks your boss used to carry, you've given your boss extra time to accept extra responsibilities for *her* superior. This helps your boss look good and should make your superior anxious to make the effort to get you what you've asked. It should also be worth money to your company since they're deriving more from *two* people: you and your boss.

3. If there was a trial period when you were hired after which your salary would be adjusted, point out that the deadline has arrived.

4. Indicate exactly how your past efforts have helped the company earn or save money. Profit is the purpose of business. Have you suggested plans or significant effort that raised earnings or cut costs in purchasing, selling, productivity, procedures, product ideas, technical improvement? If so, you have certainly contributed to the company's profits. You can therefore logically expect an appropriate increase for yourself.

5. Use possible future contributions. A philosopher once wrote that present gratitude is largely based on expectations of future favours. Stimulate that present gratitude by listing ideas for future money-making, cost-cutting, problem-solving programmes you've been thinking about. Mention that you're looking forward to making a success of the XYZ and ABC projects you've recently begun. What you're doing is making clear that you expect to continue growing in value to your employer.

6. If you feel you can't justify a merit increase but want only an inflation increase, say so. List the inflation rate in your area since the date of your last salary adjustment. (Your bank can tell you if you don't know.) Multiply your salary by that percentage and you will have the amount you need in order to retrieve the purchasing power you originally had.

Other important techniques

How much?

Newspaper job advertisements, and conversations with friends can help you judge the going rate in your area for your kind of work. When you meet with your boss, mention the specific amount you are seeking. Different people within the same organisation often earn very different salaries for similar jobs. Behaviour during salary negotiations is one of the important explanations. The person who asks for a specific amount (so much per week, month, or year) is more likely to receive something of value than the employee who merely requests 'a rise'. Remember, token small increments are handed out annually in many organisations. Those who are most apt to win increases that match their contributions are those who name specific sums. If you want both a merit and inflation increase, itemise them separately.

The right attitude

Never apologise or babble about how difficult it is for you to discuss money. If you seem to doubt your right to a higher salary, it makes it easy for your superiors to insist it's impossible to give it to you at this time. A gracious thank you is appropriate when your new salary is agreed upon, but don't gush. If you receive an increase, it's because you're giving them their money's worth.

The right timing

If possible, ask for your rise when you're surrounded by a positive aura generated by some job triumph. After you complete a successful project is an excellent time. A day or so after you've volunteered for or accepted a new responsibility is another propitious moment. 'Strike while the iron is hot' got to be a hoary maxim because it verbalises an eternal truth about human nature. If you don't act when they're first appreciating your increased efforts, management will quickly accept them as the status quo and resist paying you extra for them.

In choosing your opportunity, you must also take your boss's life into consideration. If she or he has just had a serious personal or business disappointment, you'll probably be engulfed in the generalised depression and anger he or she is feeling. Not a good time. The ideal week, if it comes along, says motivational psychologist Dr Ernest Dichter, is after your superior has enjoyed an important success. Psychologists have discovered that success makes people feel and behave generously. If it is an important success, it does even more. It often produces an internal pressure – an unconscious *need* to propitiate fate – to share the success by passing some of it on to others.

Threats

Many people ask 'Should I say that I must get the rise or I'm going to have to leave?' Never threaten. It antagonises the person you're talking to and makes it psychologically harder for her or him to say yes. A threat can even short-circuit your discussion and turn it from your salary to your departure. Your attitude and theme should be that you enjoy working here, definitely want to remain, and could we talk about adjusting your pay?

Only when it is unfortunately true do you mention that you will be forced to leave if your salary isn't adjusted by a certain amount. Even then, explain the situation calmly and emphasise that you are reluctant to move elsewhere because you are happy here. Important fact: Needing a rise is *not* a reason for requesting one. Your request must be based on one or more of the six points above. Conversely, be prepared to counter any old-fashioned talk from your employer about 'a single woman like you not *needing* that big a salary' or 'since you have a husband with a good job, you don't *need* the money.'

Point out that need is never used to set salaries for male employees. No boss ever tells a bachelor or man with a working wife 'You don't need the money.' Men's salaries are based on their responsibilities and their performance. Since the men in the organisation are being paid for performance, not need, indicate that you expect the organisation to pay women (including you) on performance, not need.

CHAPTER 24.

Seven ways to hurry your boss into promoting you

You can't learn to swim in the middle of a desert and you can't get a promotion unless you're in a job situation where promotions exist.

Dead end versus career path

Millions of good jobs are dead ends. They are good jobs because the work is steady, working conditions are pleasant, and salaries and benefits are satisfactory. But they are not good jobs for people who are interested in moving up.

If you can't see two or three promotion positions immediately in line above you that you can compete for, you are in a dead end. Sure, every organisation has numerous high-level positions. *The point is, do people in the company go from jobs like yours into those higher positions?* If the answer is no, it doesn't matter how hard you work and how efficient you are. You're in a job rut instead of a career path. Since there isn't any 'up' to go to, you can't go up!

Most clerical jobs are dead ends. Often to escape you have to move sideways or even slightly down before you can start going up. One woman who was a well-paid secretary realised that secretaries in her company received annual rises but

156

were never promoted. She took a cut in salary to join the production department as a trainee. But now she is on a career path to assistant production manager. Then either with this employer or another she can go on to production manager. Another woman who was doing clerical work for the sales department of her company learned enough to have herself shifted sideways into a career path by becoming a sales representative. With experience, she can move into sales management.

Many organisations will try to lure you into a dead-end job with the promise that 'After a few years when you've learned about the company, we'll transfer you to a job with promotion opportunities.' Experienced management consultants warn you against believing it, a management change means you are forgotten. If you are not able to rely on your own perform-ance to progress, your chances for promotion are very doubtful.

Creating a promotion

It's a common mistake to believe there has to be an 'opening' that you can be promoted to. Some employment experts believe that as many as 30 per cent of all good jobs don't exist until the right person comes along and the job is created. You can sometimes help your employers see the need to create a better job for you by turning yourself into the company expert on something. A woman in a small industrial town recently escaped from her dead-end job that way. She realised that no one in her company knew the environmental requirements for the area. She also recognised that the town's civic groups would soon begin pressuring about waste pouring from the generating-plant smokestack. She began collecting information on pollution laws and solutions from local and national officials. Then she began sending the information to company executives who needed to know these things. When the community did press, she was the natural choice for the newly created company job of Director of Community Relations.

This brings up a key question: 'If I aim for promotion by

expanding my work responsibilities, won't the boss object?' A *Harvard Business Review* analysis suggests that every organisation has 'corridors of indifference', areas that no one in the organisation is really involved in. In these areas you can expand your influence without meeting resistance. Management professor and consultant Andrew H. Souerwine believes that 'People build up feelings that bosses care more than they actually do, that bosses would somehow be shocked, angered, or threatened if subordinates went ahead and did things on their own.' Done with a sense of responsibility and concern for helping people in power positions as well as ourselves, he says such actions are usually successful and a good way to a promotion.

Balancing your credentials

As a young woman in the first decade or so of your career, you are in an ideal position to develop balanced credentials. At this stage, 'What will I learn from this job? What kinds of better jobs will it qualify me for?' can be more important questions than 'Which job pays more?' A job with high starting salary that channels you into a narrow speciality that can become a dead end can be a poor choice. Now too is the time to fill out your knowledge weaknesses. If you were the boss, would you promote you? Or do you recognise you should know more about basic supervisory principles and techniques, budgeting, computers, record-keeping, marketing techniques? Whatever the kind of job you are interested in rising to, find out what standard experience and academic credentials are required for it. Then get them. (Your company may have day release or other training programmes that can help you.) Next make sure your boss realises you've filled your knowledge gaps and that you're now well prepared to move ahead.

Act the part

It's a business truism that to get ahead you have to dress like the people on the level above you. By looking the part, you make it easy for your superiors to see you as a candidate for the job. You must also *act* the part. Most people direct all their working attention to their narrow specific task and never consider the company's or department's main goals. When you use your spoken and written reports to your superior to indicate you're aware of and are contributing to the overall goals, you stand out. For example, you may be a computer operator in a data processing company. When you begin sending the company owner ideas on how the computer work can be performed to cut time costs and/or raise customer confidence and company profits, you transform your image. The big purpose of your company is getting and keeping customers and generating profits. You are showing an ability to produce ideas for these top goals. You therefore become someone who seems a suitable candidate to operate at the higher levels of the company where these goals are dealt with regularly.

Keep your eye on the doughnut, not on the hole

You must spend time figuring out what types of achievement are rewarded in your company and which are regarded as meaningless. A woman engineer hired by a small firm for a research and development department spent the first four months weeding out and developing new record-keeping systems for the disorganised, overgrown research files. She never had a chance to try for promotion. She lost her job. Her boss was totally unimpressed with the new smooth-functioning record system. He wanted a research and development department that produced ideas for new products.

Where the power is

To win a promotion, you must understand who has the power to approve or prevent it. Then you must please and impress the people with the power. It varies from job to job. Perhaps your department head makes decisions for some positions, but for others it's your boss's boss who decides.

Every organisation has two power charts, the published

one and the invisible one. Since the invisible chart profoundly affects who gets promotions and rises, it is well worth your while to learn about it. To start with, never assume that the person with the title and power actually *uses* the power. The president of the company may concentrate on public affairs or major marketing decisions and leave personnel promotion to the number-three person on the chart.

Some signs of invisible power: the person who supplies reliable information. Among all the daily grapevine talk, who often comes out with the facts? That person either has power or is very close to the source of power. Who has social contacts with top executives through spouses or mutual activities in political, community, or religious organisations? That person has the boss's attention in influential ways and times. Anyone with relatives or former bosses in the executive ranks may have a sponsor or mentor who will pull her or him up – and you too if you impress that privileged co-worker. Anyone who is currently involved in an office romance with a person in power, even if it's true some day the romance may come to a sticky end. At the moment, though, the lesser person in the duo commands considerable power in the organisation through the romance. You can either harness this power duo to work for you or perhaps be steam-rollered by it.

Talk up

As women have moved into full-time careers, employment experts have discovered that too many women operate on the theory that 'If I'm efficient, I'll be noticed and rewarded.' It's not true. There are always exceptions, but the typical boss's attitude is 'If subordinates don't ask for a promotion or a rise, they must be perfectly satisfied, so why stir things up?' Even if a boss has a more positive attitude, bosses are busy people. *You* may realise you have credentials for a better job but the boss is busy thinking about her own problems. She may not recognise you're well suited for the promotion. Explain your qualifications. Ask for the promotion.

If you are passed over for a promotion you thought you

deserved, go to your supervisor and *pleasantly* ask what you need to do to be considered for the next suitable opening. Then listen. Also ask if you may draw your supervisor's attention to your strong points. Discuss them and leave a list of them. Next time there's an opening, chances are your boss will be aware of you as a candidate. If you've been tactful and presented your case well, your boss may even feel you're owed something right now for having been ignored for this promotion – and you may be given a rise, a better title, or some other advantage.

CHAPTER **25.**

What the job-testers are looking for – and how to give them the answers they want

This chapter discusses selection/promotion job tests. In addition to selection/promotion job tests there are two other kinds of job tests you can take:

1. *Skill Tests.* You're asked to type a letter, take and read back shorthand, or programme a computer. Used by employers to judge your skill competence.

2. *Career Guidance Tests.* Given by career guidance organisations to help you choose a career. Usually they consist of written and oral psychological exercises. Testers are trying to develop a picture of your personality, attitudes, aptitudes, interests, emotional patterns. The only way to get useful career advice is to answer honestly.

Thousands of employers require you to take selection/ promotion tests before they will offer you a job or a promotion. The testers try to see if your personality, human relations skills, attitudes, and emotional temperament 'fit' the job. The tests are of two types: (1) a series of psychological exercises similar to career guidance exercises described above, and (2) 'assessment games'. For assessment sessions you're asked to play business games where you carry out various tasks while testers watch and judge you. In these games you might have to assign work to subordinates, solve a departmental budget problem, cope with an irate phone call from a customer, make a presentation. Since you won't be offered the job unless you do well on these written-oral and/or assessment problems, you'll be anxious to compile a good score.

What the selection/promotion job tests mean

Some distinguished industrial psychologists and other experts doubt that selection/promotion job tests mean very much. They point out there is insufficient evidence proving that the tests do what they claim to do. Little evidence, for instance, that examinations for managerial ability really do pick the top managerial talent or that tests for problem-solving do predict real-life skills.

Despite the doubts about the tests' validity, more and more employers are adopting them. Many use them only to fill supervisory and executive positions. Others insist on them for applicants for nearly all jobs. Employers depend on selection/promotion tests to decide which people to hire, which slots to assign employees to, and which people to promote.

The employers have their reasons. When they use the tests, they can say hiring is based on examination results, not on interviewer judgments. This protects them from employment-discrimination lawsuits. The tests also satisfy the fervent human need to pass the buck. If interviews alone are used and a new employee turns out to be incompetent, the executive who did the hiring may be blamed. But when tests are used as the basis for hiring and the new employee turns out to be incompetent, everyone is safe. It's the tests' fault.

What to expect

At the start you're usually told 'There are no right or wrong answers. Just be yourself and give your own opinion.'

Of course, there really are preferred answers and your replies will be fed into the computer and marked. The 'correct' answers represent the ideal pattern of personality, attitudes, and IQ that the tester believes necessary *for that particular job. Each occupation has a different ideal pattern.* It is created from answers given by people who previously held that job. The ideal personality pattern for sales supervisor will be more outgoing, more group-oriented than the pattern for bank examiner. The ideal social worker personality pattern will be more helpful, more concerned with the opinions of others, less aggressive than the executive's pattern. A brokerage executive will almost surely be required to be more conservative and less imaginative than an advertising executive.

The final judgment about you will not be based on any single answer you give. It will be determined by how closely your overall answers resemble the tester's ideal candidate.

Giving them the answers they want

Your chances of being offered the position depend on how accurately you figure out what characteristics the testers are seeking for the job – and then give them the answers they want. Whether you *want* to go to the trouble of figuring out what the testers are looking for and then making yourself seem like that kind of person is something only you can decide. *But the question of being honest isn't really involved.*

Remember, the testers' ideal pattern was developed from answers given by people who have held that job. Since the previous jobholders were human, they doubtless also tried to supply answers they thought were 'proper'. If, for example, they were office managers, they tried to claim the virtues they *thought* an office manager ought to possess. Therefore, since your answers are *not* being compared to honest replies, honesty ceases to be involved. If you do decide you want the job, you then might as well do what you can to help yourself.

The testers are aware of this nearly universal desire to help yourself and they build into tests various traps to try to catch faked attitudes. One of their favourites is the use of words like *never* and *always*. You see this in questions like 'I have never been tempted to take anything that wasn't mine' or 'I always control my temper no matter how unreasonable other people are.' In general, you are wise to present yourself as having good attitudes – honesty, emotionally stable, and the like. But claiming 100 per cent virtue makes the tester suspicious that you are too good to be true. They will consider 100 per cent claims (which is what *always* and *never* are) as faked. Therefore, the 'right' answer to both questions is false. (They make no allowance for the fact that you really and truly may never have been tempted to take anything that wasn't yours. Mark the question 'true' and you'll be scored as falsifying.)

The tests also have scattered through them a variety of questions that keep asking about the same idea using different words. The testers are trying to see if you contradict yourself. If you do answer the same type of question in very different ways, it counts as faked and counts against you. It works like this: In one battery of tests where 'seriousness versus easygoing' attitudes are among the characteristics being judged you find multiple questions dealing with it, such as:

On page 4: 'The effort taken in planning ahead (a) is never wasted, (b) in between, (c) is not worth it.'
On page 5: 'I live for the "here and now" more than most people do (a) true, (b) uncertain, (c) false.'

To be consistent you should have chosen the 'seriousness' answers both times: page 4, a; page 5, c. Our informing you that multiple questions on the *same* characteristics are part of almost every personality test gives you the advance notice you need to look out for them and recognize them.

Right answers, wrong answers

Though the following guidelines are generally true, they are not foolproof. For every suggestion mentioned below, someone somewhere can find exceptions. Different testers may interpret the same answers differently. And individual companies may be searching for personality types that would amaze you. One distinguished book publisher counts it against sales representatives if they have literary interests. A major drug corporation that sells to hospitals and doctors rejects you if you have a very high IQ.

In general, though, when being appraised for supervisory or executive positions, keep in mind that companies want executives to be driven by a need to achieve. If you work more for the pay and what it will buy than for the pure sense of achievement, don't admit it. Neither should you suggest there is such a thing as enough money. Questions like these will test you:

1. What would you most like to do if you had worked long and hard enough to become a millionaire? You're offered a choice of retiring and enjoying life, developing yourself intellectually, creating a worthwhile philanthropic project, or starting a new business and making more money. (The last is the 'right' answer.)

2. Choose one (a) I like to help my friends when they are in trouble, or (b) I like to do my very best in whatever I undertake. (The achiever's answer is b.)

3. Choose as many of the following life purposes as greatly interest you:
   a. to have interesting and important work.
   b. to inherit a million dollars.
   c. to be brave, truthful, loyal, and kind.
   d. to travel widely.
   e. to have good looks and personality.

If you want to sit behind an executive desk, the only goal on that list that will tempt you is a. (The million dollars bore you because you're inheriting instead of earning them.)

It is dangerous to acknowledge cultural interests of any kind. In the tester's eyes they often mark you as unfit for executive life. For example, from the battery of questions used by one of the largest of American employers:

'Are our modern industrial and scientific developments signs of a greater degree of civilisation than those attained by a previous society – the Greeks, for example?'

Select the Greeks and the computer will say you are unsuited to be an executive and ought to be a decorator.

In addition to 'achievement,' people who want to become executives should choose test answers that show they are:

- Tough-minded rather than tender-minded, the better to hire, fire, confront, and pursue objectives.
- Sociable on the surface but really cool and reserved. Thought to make for better administrators.
- Bright, high on abstract thinking.
- Calm and stable temperamentally. Excitability is seen as apprehensiveness, which is seen as guilt, which is seen as neurosis.
- Practical versus imaginative. Depends on the position you're after and the industry it's in. Obviously more jobs in advertising than in banking will allow for imagination. But you'd better have a good dollop of practicality.
- Suspicious versus trusting. A high opinion of human nature will count against you. While being careful not to appear paranoid, you should be somewhat suspicious rather than trusting. How will you outwit and keep from being outwitted otherwise?

When the testers come to your personal life – for any job – admitting to rebellion against your father is out of the question. To the testers the company represents a father figure. If you report rebellion against your real father, you will be considered unable to follow directives and unable to adjust to corporate life. At the same time you must be very careful not to appear emotionally dependent on your parents.

The testers may try to understand your relations with your parents, your emotional stability, and your life attitudes by asking you to draw pictures, complete sentences, and tell stories about picture cards and ink blots.

Drawings

For all kinds of jobs, when you are asked to draw people, keep these guidelines in mind: full face is judged to be better than profile. If you leave out a part of the body, to the tester it may mean you are repelled by it. Aggressiveness and power drives are thought to be shown by the strength and quality of your lines. Overdressing your creation is a sign of vanity. The facial expression reflects your own life outlook. To a tester a button nose means immaturity, emphasised nostrils signal 'temper'. Limply hanging arms indicate indecisiveness, arms that go out and back in and feet pointed in opposite directions may mean you are afraid to tangle with life as it is. Buttons on clothing are an unmitigated disaster interpreted as your mother didn't love you and now you are an emotional mess. The drawing should be approximately in the middle of the page, reasonably large, and for heaven's sake don't put a ground line as a horizon. They'll say you're insecure. If you draw both a man and woman, the tester may see the one with the larger head as your choice for 'the superior sex'.

Sentence completion

Another technique the testers use involves giving you the beginning of a sentence and asking you to finish it. By your answers they hope to discover 'the real you'. In order to project a real you who is fit for the job, keep in mind the qualities you believe are needed for that job and answer accordingly.

For someone seeking a supervisory or executive position the following could be samples of good sentence completion answers:

> *When I make a mistake, I* . . . try to find out why and correct it.
> *Working with others makes me* . . . feel responsible for their growth.
> *When they said I couldn't do it, I* . . . said it should be tried.
> *When everything goes wrong, I* . . . try to isolate the cause and create order.

When someone gets the better of me, I . . . am irritated but plan for the next time.

I often wish . . . to do a great job.

Working alone is . . . just that, lonely.

In getting to know people, I . . . believe all people have some assets.

Stories about picture cards

At these storytelling sessions they may say 'This is a test of imagination. Make your accounts as dramatic as possible.' Don't be misled! They're not interested in your imaginative powers. They are attempting to judge the same list of personality characteristics as did the other tests. By directing you to concentrate on drama they hope to strip away your guard and thereby discover that elusive 'true you'. As you tell your stories, the tester will be concentrating on what the heroines in your account do.

They will see the heroines and their behaviour as a reflection *of your own private image of yourself*. If your heroines get into trouble and are constantly having to be rescued by others – rather than by their own calm decisions and actions – you will be said to be a weak, dependent person. If your heroines have problems controlling their emotions and directing their lives intelligently, you will be thought to be that kind of person. Overall, then, you are going to be careful that the heroines in your tales behave only in ways that illustrate the qualities you believe are needed to succeed at the job you want.

When applying for a job with lots of stress – police officer, flight controller, social worker, etc – tell stories about women who are low in excitability, high in self-assurance, confidence, and self-control, serious rather than impulsive, conservative rather than experimental.

For sales-representative positions the ideal heroine will be acquisitive, aggressive, persistent, shrewd, independent, selfish, impatient of supervision, and interested in people only enough to use them for her own gain. Above all, she must be money-hungry, anxious to sell because she thinks it is the best route to big income. (Being interested in selling because you like people or like to travel will *lose* you the job.)

Arithmetic and detail skills often count against a sales-rep candidate. Good sales personnel are thought to be impatient, to do poorly on anything that requires detailed planning. On sentence-completion tests good sales candidates cover up and tell as little as possible. (Being self-revealing would put them at a disadvantage with customers.) In imaginative tales they might tell of a salesperson who is in conflict with a superior, becomes annoyed, and takes her case right over her superior's head to the big boss. This is the kind of person testers believe will do a good, tough, competitive sales job.

For a sales *executive* position (sales manager, branch manager); your ideal heroine will be a salesperson at heart with administrative qualities added. Unlike the rep she can plan and do detail work. She takes delight in making decisions, is anxious to compete and to influence others. She is assertive, a leader, a positive thinker.

Ink blot tests

You are shown ink blots made by old-fashioned liquid ink and asked what shapes, pictures, activities you see. Testers believe that what you see in the grey spaces of the blots reflect your sensitivity and understanding of people. Don't observe too much in the grey, though, or they'll tag you as anxious. Altogether in the black, white, and grey be sure to see quite a lot. An inhibited, rigid person is found out by the small number of total responses.

Your intellectual ability is judged by the number of overall pictures the total ink blot suggests to you and the number and type of human activities you observe. The more active the humans are the more mature you are. Pushing, pulling, jumping, working humans are all splendid. Content, smiling humans are to be avoided at all costs. They may make testers believe that deep-down you don't really like yourself. One of the best ink-blot answers involves combining grey tones and a form into a realistic three-dimensional image such as 'looking down a tree-lined street'. This indicates, they believe, a person with good insight into himself or herself and others.

Assessment tests

These tests, in which you act out job games, are used most often for management positions. The games are attempts to judge your management skills: problem analysis, judgment, decisiveness, leadership, interpersonal sensitivity, initiative, and organisational planning.

The in-tray game is very popular. For it you pretend you've suddenly been named to replace another executive. The company president has asked you to go through your predecessor's in-tray where some thirty separate important problems have been accumulating. You have to decide quickly about a new company development programme, shortage of clerical help, complaints about promotions, personnel hiring problems, a questionable travel voucher, imminent deadline for next year's department budget, and so forth.

To demonstrate good managerial ability, quickly separate items by priority, category, and problem. Those who fail to do this are sometimes horrified to discover that a later item in the basket changes facts or dates for problems they've already decided. There are no right or wrong solutions to each of the in-tray problems. You're being judged on how you deal with your new superiors and subordinates, how you plan, delegate, and organize your work, the work standards you set for others, and whether you demonstrate those characteristics (discussed previously) that good managers are thought to need.

In another popular game a leaderless group is turned loose to arrive at a group decision. You'll be watched for assertiveness, ability to make your point, ability to take hold of situations and lead. Observers agree that assessment exercises usually penalise the non-assertive personality. Throughout all games and interaction with the assessors, a firm handshake, social poise, use of first names, and good eye contact will usually be deemed assets.

In another assessment game you may be a newly appointed manager who must decide whether to go ahead with a research project. You have five minutes to prepare questions about the project, fifteen minutes to ask them. No matter how skilful your questioning, when you finish you'll be told you didn't obtain a piece of important information. The staff person may then try to convince you to change your decision because of the new facts. You're not being judged on whether you change your mind or not. They're interested in your ability to use all the information to justify your final decision effectively, to demonstrate an ability to seek vital information and then analyse it intelligently.

Job testers like to discourage you from trying to outguess them. 'People who try it get confused and do poorly,' they say.

But how in the world could the testers possibly know? The faking examples they notice are those that are botched. The people who succeed – who *do* outguess the testers – *get* the jobs they're after. They're certainly not going to come back and tell the testers all about it!

CHAPTER 26.

Dos and don'ts for succeeding after a promotion

Your chances of being promoted have never been better. Despite sex-discrimination problems that still exist women are currently winning more promotions than ever before in business history.

When your turn comes to be a supervisor, here are some important dos and don'ts that will help you succeed.

Don't make sweeping changes during the beginning weeks

New bosses have all the cards stacked in their favour, says Joel Moses, manager of Personnel Research for AT&T, the large American corporation. The people the new boss is going to supervise will be anxious to be friends because they know their own jobs depend on good relations with their superior. Furthermore, says Dr Moses, new supervisors have 'job charisma' operating for them. The very fact that some-one has won the position and has the job title usually impresses people and produces an initial favourable impression.

Dr Moses explains that when you first take over you build on this initial positive reaction toward you by saying little and simply following established routine. If your predecessor was a success, you are probably starting with workers who know what is required of them. If your predecessor was a crank or failure, you're bound to appear to everyone as an improvement. Unless you were hired to solve a crisis, making sweeping method or assignment changes when you first arrive is a serious mistake. It will ignite wildfire hostility against you as everyone begins to fear a job shakeup and threat to her or his job security. The time to start making gradual changes is when you know your people as individuals.

Don't sabotage yourself when you talk

Many women give off conflicting images. They say they want co-workers to take them seriously as competent and know-ledgeable people. But when they discuss business with co-workers they concentrate on what will make them popular rather than on what is necessary to be effective. They further weaken themselves as supervisors by letting their voices trail off when making an important point. Or they cancel out the impact of their statements by undercutting them with a nervous laugh at the end of key sentences.

Management consultant John T. Molloy points out that many newly appointed women managers sabotage their authority by ignoring the usual boss-subordinate rela-tionship and insisting 'we're all partners working together'. When subordinates then begin reacting casually to work orders, the new managers panic and complain they aren't being properly accepted by their staff. Molloy believes your success as a new manager – and good on-the-job relations with subordinates too – depends on everyone pleasantly understanding that subordinates don't work *with* you. They work *for* you.

Don't wait until you know each detail about a subject before you venture a comment

Alice G. Sargent, consultant to major corporations and specialist in managerial effectiveness, has found that women supervisors tend to be overly cautious. If they haven't totally briefed themselves on the subject, they say nothing. Since there are very few topics you can be an expert on, such an attitude can leave you looking passive and weak. Based on her research, Dr Sargent points out that the average male executive doesn't feel he needs a superior level of knowledge on a business topic before venturing a comment. She recommends that women can become more effective managers by acting in the same fashion.

Do adapt your old work friendships to the new situation

If you've been promoted over your former co-workers in your old department, you will need tact to manage the new relationships. In addition to valuing your old friendships for their own sakes, you must have the continued cooperation of your friends to keep your group producing well.

Though some of the intimate aspects, such as eating lunch together every day, may fade – or even be discouraged by company policy – you can avoid a she's-got-a-swelled-head reaction. Everyone should understand when you explain you must associate with the other supervisors if you're to learn what you're supposed to be doing and keep informed of new developments.

Most important, says Seymour J. Fader, management consultant and author of an American Management Association's basic text for supervisors, don't let your comradely feelings about your former co-workers interfere with the proper use of your authority. You can't allow yourself to waive company rules or work standards for them. If you do, your group's performance will soon falter. And, since your success depends primarily on your group's performance, you'll be heading for failure in your new position.

Do learn to delegate

New managers often mistakenly attempt to prove their worth in deadline situations by rolling up their sleeves and completing most of the work themselves. Successful managers meet deadlines by analysing the workload and delegating portions of it to others. Dale D. McConkey, corporate executive and author of the book *No-Nonsense Delegation* (Amacom), explains that to delegate successfully you must be willing to give your subordinates the authority they need to carry out an assignment. For example, don't tell your staff or secretary the details of how to set up and carry out a project. As long as they fulfil their responsibilities satisfactorily, let them develop their own work methods.

McConkey also emphasises that successful delegation depends on how a boss reacts to performance. That is, you can and should publicly credit a subordinate for delegated assignments well done. But blame when assignments miscarry is something to discuss privately with the individual.

Tasks that are often easiest and wisest to delegate include: (1) matters that keep repeating themselves; (2) job details you most dislike; (3) parts of the job you are least qualified to handle; (4) details that consume the largest chunks of your time; (5) matters for which there are set procedures to follow.

Do realise that every new female executive your company hires strengthens your position

Research by industrial psychologists indicates that although a lone man in a female-dominated business group wields considerable power, the reverse is not true. The experiments indicate that when there is only one man present, he and his ideas often are deferred to and respected just by virtue of his being the lone male. The token woman in a male-dominated group has no such good fortune. The researchers report she often has great difficulty winning respect and acceptance for her business comments and suggestions. But the researchers also discovered that women's influence with their colleagues rises significantly when the female representation in the group increases. All of which means it will help *you* achieve status and business power when you work to bring other women into positions of authority where they will attend meetings and be part of your company's executive corps.

CHAPTER 27.

How to succeed without really competing

There are no scoring norms. The text of the chapter interprets the quizzes for you.

What's your job attitude?

Which of the following describe you?
If it sounds
'a lot like me'   mark it **L**
'somewhat like me'   mark it **S**
'not at all like me'   mark it **N**

1. I am concerned about always producing at my job in a way that measures up to my standards.

2. I enjoy becoming involved in my work.

3. I get satisfaction from a completed job well done.

4. I like to feel tired and 'used' at the end of a day.

5. After I've learned what I'm supposed to do on my job, I enjoy maintaining a regular daily routine.

6. After I have mastered my job, I look around for new challenges.

7. I like to see if I can beat my old performance in doing a job better or faster or in a more efficient manner.

8. When I come to something new and different on my job, I enjoy having to figure it out.

9. After I've done a particular task well, I often get restless and start thinking 'That's fine. But now what can I go on to?'

10. I like a job that allows me to keep learning new skills.

11. The only real way I can tell how well I'm doing is by comparing my performance to other people's performance.

12. I don't like hurting other people. But I do like to be Number 1.

13. It's important to me to win when I'm competing with someone for a sale or promotion or for recognition.

14. I've heard a lot of women say they don't like to be competitive. Being competitive, including stepping on others if it's necessary, is the way the system works. In order to succeed, I guess I'll have to act that way too.

What job fears do you have?

Use the same L, S, N code for marking.

1. Are you worried that you won't ever obtain the kind of job you want or earn the salary you want because you're not competitive enough?

2. Are you afraid you'll never be good enough at office politics to beat the competition?

3. Do you think men have built-in odds in their favour because men have a childhood history of learning to be competitive through their sports activities?

4. Do you believe women have built-in odds against them because they're 'afraid of success'?

5. Because of job fears 1, 2, 3, and 4, have you decided you're automatically out of the running and that it's futile to hope for significant career success?

But I'm not really competitive

If you're a 'nice person', a civilised human being, you may feel your chances for career success are poor. After all, hasn't every one of us heard that to succeed you have to be a ruthless competitor and a first-rate office politician? Over the last few years as the print and electronic media broadcast this message at us, your reaction may have been 'If that's the way I have to behave to make it, then count me out.' You may have added 'Even if I were willing to go for other people's jugular, I get so wrapped up in my job that I keep forgetting about politicking.'

Until now, the usual 'expert's' response to your viewpoint has been 'You're exhibiting the "female tendency" of thinking that hard work and high performance are going to get you somewhere.' But now a study by two distinguished psychologists, Robert L. Helmreich of the University of Texas and Janet T. Spence of the Center for Advanced Studies in the Behavioral Sciences, has produced the startling conclusion that a highly competitive nature may not be a necessity for career success. Quite the opposite: a highly competitive nature may be a hindrance.

What then do you need to succeed? Are you ready for a shock? It seems that old-fashioned virtues of hard work and high performance can take you far.

Dr Spence and Dr Helmreich point out that Americans, especially, have usually thought that being competitive was the single essential characteristic that led to success. 'We believed,' they say, 'that there might be a combination of behaviour characteristics involved, not just the single trait. Success might be the result of a mixture of the following: how much you enjoy working hard and keeping busy. How interested you are in mastering new skills. How competitive you are. And, do you worry about other people resenting your success?'

Through a list of thirty-two questions they devised, they tested the achievement motivation of groups of college students, businessmen,* and scientists. Based on the answers, they divided people into four groups:

Group 1: high work, high mastery,† low competitive
Group 2: low work, low mastery, high competitive
Group 3: high work, high mastery, high competitive
Group 4: low work, low mastery, low competitive

Next they ranked the achievements of the students, businessmen, and scientists. Success was defined by the students' college grades, the businessmen's income, and the professional stature of the scientists' research.

After all their computations, computer printouts, and final graphing, one fact was clear: Group 1, high in work habits, high in mastery, and low in competitiveness was the most successful. Below it, groups 2 and 3 were about equally successful; Group 4 lagged significantly behind 2 and 3.

Exactly why Group 3, which appears to have everything (high work, high mastery, high competitiveness), should have a success record about equal to 2 but not as successful as 1 is something the psychologists have not yet investigated. Consequently they are reluctant to comment. 'The significant thing,' says Dr Helmreich, 'is what we do have data on: concentrating on work and performance (mastery) and *not* concentrating on beating out others seems to lead to success.'

Dr Spence offers a verbal picture of the behaviour produced by each of the characteristics: work, mastery, competitiveness. In her descriptions she clarified the differences between being strong only in work habits but not strong in mastery. (To be part of the successful Group 1 required strength in both.)

The high-work men and women put forth lots of effort, do the job well. They have personal standards for their perform-

---

* Though the groups of students and scientists were composed of both men and women, the businesspeople were only men.
† Mastery in terms of performance, skills.

ance and live up to them. They master what is required and develop a regular routine for handling daily responsibilities. Though they are valued employees, they are probably not going to rise very far because they produce few new ideas and they dislike challenges. (In the 'What's Your Job Attitude?' quiz at the beginning of this chapter, questions 1–5 deal with your attitude toward 'work'.)

For the high-mastery person, working is not just meeting her own standards. She enjoys challenging tasks and trying to solve difficult problems. She is constantly on the lookout for ways to improve her performance and to learn new skills. If she finds herself developing a predictable daily routine, she starts looking around for something new to tackle, to learn, to master. 'What am I going to move on to next?' is her perpetual attitude. The high-mastery person is in a kind of competition with herself, striving to become better. This self-competition absorbs so much of her attention that, for her, winning over someone else becomes a marginal issue. (In the quiz, questions 6–10 deal with your attitude toward 'mastery'.)

The highly competitive person compared herself and her performance to other people and theirs. The level of her performance is not her major interest. Her concern lies with 'winning' and with 'being better than the others'. This can translate into satisfaction with sloppy work if the others are even sloppier. During her school days this kind of person might earn 62 on a test. If everyone else in the class received a grade below 60, she would be perfectly satisfied. True, she barely passed the test and she hadn't mastered the information, but she did better than the others and that's all that concerns her. As she sees it, if something is important enough and the only way she can come out first is by 'knocking someone over', she may do so. (In the quiz, questions 11–14 deal with your attitude toward 'competitiveness'.)

The difference between the two kinds of competitiveness – competing with yourself and competing with others – is crucial. When people say 'I'm just not competitive', 99.9 per cent of the time they really mean 'I don't like competing against others.' (See 1 and 2 in the job fears quiz.)

The value of this study is that it shows us that it is possible to be competitive in a way that many of us *are comfortable* with. We're also competitive when we compete with our own past performance. Furthermore, it's this kind of self-competition, according to the Helmreich-Spence research, that promotes career success.

Do both sexes have an equal chance?

More good news. Despite what you may have heard or read elsewhere, there doesn't appear to be a man's route or a woman's route to success. Rather, there appears to be a 'people's route' that both men and women gravitate to.

Since the successful Group 1 pattern depends on hard work and high performance, women's childhood seems to prepare them about as well as boys are prepared. 'Yes, there were small differences. Women as a group (individuals varied) showed up as higher in work, men as a group higher in mastery. But similarities between the sexes are more impressive than the differences.' Only in competitiveness were men 'markedly higher'. Yet we've seen that this is not the advantage it's been thought to be and may even be a disadvantage.

What of fears 3 and 4 in the 'What Job Fears Do You Have?' quiz?

'3. Do you think men have built-in odds in their favour because men have a childhood history of learning to be competitive through their sports activities?'

This so-called advantage gained by a youth devoted to team sport has received wide coverage lately, notably in *The Managerial Woman* by Margaret Hennig and Anne Jardim. During the interview for this book we specifically asked about 'the managerial woman' ideas. 'Learning to work together for a common team goal may be valuable. We don't know. We haven't researched that. But our data do indicate that learning a competitive attitude through childhood sports rivalry is *not* important. In fact, as we've seen, it may be a handicap because it may cause you to concentrate on superficial "winning" rather than on constantly raising your own level of performance.'

You might be tempted at this point to remark 'But what's the difference? If you win, you're successful, aren't you?'

'No,' say Helmreich and Spence. 'Winning the job or promotion over someone else isn't going to help you if you haven't mastered the skills you need to stay there.'

As for fear 4 from the quiz: 'Do you believe women have built-in odds against them because they're "afraid of success"?'

The fear-of-success phenomenon has been widely discussed and written about, especially in women's publications. The concept is based, of course, on Matina Horner's famous psychological experiments that were supposed to indicate that women were so worried about others resenting their success that the women fled from their opportunities.

Since Dr Horner's 1968 experiments, many other equally respected researchers have attempted to duplicate her results and have failed. What many of these researchers report is that *both* men and women seem to realise that success may cause envy and resentment. As a result, some men decide that others' jealousy is too high a price to pay, just as some women do. In short, some men are afraid of success and so are some women. And there are women as well as men who are not afraid of success. The pattern appears to be *human*, not male or female.

The Helmreich and Spence research takes our knowledge a step further. In their achievement motivation questionnaire they included questions that probed sensitivity to other people's opinions, specifically others' attitude towards your *achievements*. Their results: the average woman in their study was slightly *less* concerned about other people's reaction to her success than was the average man. Or, to put it the other way around: When it comes to 'fear of success', the men in the Helmreich–Spence experiments exhibited slightly more of it than the women did!

Is that all it takes?

Does all this mean that hard work and mastery of the required knowledge and skills are a guarantee of success? No, it doesn't.

The students, businessmen, and scientists who were tested by Helmreich and Spence were selected as being approximately equal in intelligence and education. The researchers were attempting to discover which achievement motivations produce the most success among people who are equally talented.

They point out that in addition to your own efforts 'basic intelligence, education, luck, being in the right place at the right time – would Jerry Ford have been president if not for Nixon and Watergate? – and yes, office politics will always influence the final, overall result.'

Now that you know that your personal self-competition/hard work approach is the basic necessity for success, you may find it worthwhile to round out your abilities by acquiring office-politics knowledge.

As for those who have read this far and say 'But none of this sounds like me. I don't seem to fit any of the patterns except loser Group 4. Yet I'm already quite successful and I just know I'm going to do even better,' the Helmreich–Spence study does have something for you too. Having demolished the monolithic view of success – as something caused by the single characteristic of competitiveness – and proved the existence of other reliable routes, they thereby establish for everyone a permanently more open-ended view of the subject.

The truth is that besides work, mastery, competitiveness, and personal unconcern, many other influential – and as yet unrecognised – factors may exist, for example self-discipline. Someone who has no real love of hard work or of difficult, new challenges may be sufficiently disciplined to work hard enough and well enough to achieve her private goals. Still others may be deeply committed to goals that interpret success in terms of happiness, ethics, religion, or service, and thus cannot be judged by the ordinary materialistic success standards of income, status, and power.

Spence and Helmreich say: 'We do not say we have covered it all. We have a more complete model of factors on paper and when we have worked further and developed these, we will have a greater ability to make individual predictions of success.'

Do you still have time?

Perhaps you've never really thought much about trying for a successful career. Can you plug in now at this point in your life? Though Dr Helmreich and Dr Spence believe that many people adopt the successful high work/high mastery/low competitiveness behaviour very early in life, 'maybe way back in primary school,' there seems to be no logical reason to think you can't initiate the cycle at any age. Everyone is acquainted with a few people who drifted through school, drifted through a few jobs, and suddenly seemed to catch fire. 'Wherever it starts the successes that are produced are very reinforcing. If you get all kinds of rewards from working hard and mastering new skills, it plays back on itself and keeps feeding itself.'

Many young women who began with no real career goals have now had the experience of suddenly finding themselves excited about their jobs. As they do work hard, master the necessary skills, and begin winning career successes, they find they are setting in motion their own personal, constantly renewing cycle of effort and reward, which leads to success and more success.

CHAPTER **28.**

Where the promotion opportunities will be: from now to 1990

Your promotion opportunities in the next decade will depend on your having the right skills and being in the right places. The Warwick Manpower Research Group, forecasting employment in Britain for the first half of the 1980s, suggested that throughout industry there would be increases in managerial, professional and technical employment. This, the Group said, reflects growing organisational and technical complexity. These jobs need more training. They also need new training (who could operate a word processor 10 years ago?). Training in tomorrow's skills is the best way of ensuring your career.

Do I need a degree?

Yes, if you are interested in managerial or administrative jobs. Ten or fifteen years ago an employer might have hired somebody with A Levels for many of these jobs. Now there are so many graduates available that employers require a degree, for the same jobs. In many cases they even demand a post-graduate degree.

Some experts believe that because of the trend towards more schooling there will eventually be more graduates than graduate-level positions to fill. But look at it this way. Without a degree you will find it more difficult to compete for managerial and administrative jobs. With it – in good times and bad – you will have an excellent chance of being one of the lucky ones. Of course, a degree is an entry requirement into law, medicine, accounting, dentistry, engineering and other professions.

Where do I look for the promotion opportunity I want?

Most of the jobs come up as people retire, die, quit or are promoted. So a replacement job is likely to be your best opportunity. But there are new jobs too, especially in the newer technological fields, and newer industries.

Over the past 10 years, one of the most remarkable changes in Britain is where the jobs have gone. More and more of them – especially in fields like computers, which are also employing a lot of women – are in smaller towns outside the great traditional cities. As people have moved their homes out from the big conurbations, so have whole industries moved, or sprung up.

Some of the firms are small ones. In general, the larger the organisation the better the opportunities for women. But don't underestimate these new businesses. They are young, probably less hidebound, and some of them are going to grow. You could grow with them. And work in pleasant surroundings too.

A booming town or new suburb can provide many good positions. Career opportunities multiply with the opening of each new retail store, professional office, service business, and government agency branch to serve the growing population.

Even so, any metropolitan area with hundreds of thousands of employed people is and will continue to be the ideal job-hunting location for most kinds of positions. Job hunters are often misled by statistics which say that some town expects a job increase of 20 per cent during the 1980s. A 20 per cent increase can be produced by adding a mere 200 jobs to a town with a thousand jobs. And 200 new jobs is not a lot if you are looking for employment. But in a big city, where there are a million jobs, an addition of 20,000 new positions will work out to 'only a 2 per cent increase'. Yet if you're job-hunting, that 2 per cent offers you a lot of chances – plus all those replacement openings.

What else should I know?

Constantly keep track of how changing conditions are affecting your job and your job-skills. Don't wait until you are forced to change. When you read a report in a newspaper or a magazine forecasting automation or expanding developments in your work, that's the time to start acting. Time to train to operate the new machines or to move into the managerial or better jobs the expanding situation provides. If you dawdle, you will find that when you are forced to act there will be a flood of others like you scrambling and competing for the better jobs that everyone has finally learned of and trained for.

How technology affects the kinds of high-quality jobs available to you can be seen in computer and word processing occupations. The demand is growing for people skilled in the new console and auxiliary equipment, with fewer people being needed for the lower-income keypunch work. Similarly, dictating machines will limit the number of shorthand-typist jobs. But demand for secretaries skilled in automated word-processing equipment is increasing.

Population trends also affect the kinds of better quality jobs available for you. With the drop in the birth rate there are fewer jobs for youth services but a rising demand for those trained in retirement and old-age service. The same birth rate decline means less demand for teachers from elementary grades all the way through college, a condition that is expected to last through the 1990s.

Good business conditions, of course, stimulate many kinds of jobs. Even a recession, though, can be good for *some* businesses if you know where to look. Anything to do with repair or do-it-yourself usually thrives as people make-do with what they have instead of buying new. Similarly, though holiday resorts may suffer during poor economic times, sales of products related to home entertainment rise. For example, at-home family games of all kinds usually become popular.

Other excellent jobs of all kinds are tied to government contracts. Should you hear of a sudden demand for certain skills, check whether employment depends on government purchasing. If so, this demand may not last long. By the time you complete a course of study for that occupation, government contracts may have vanished, taking with them the jobs and long-term career potential. This has happened in various engineering and other technical fields over the past few decades. However, sometimes plans for permanent government spending can be your best guide to a successful career.

The impact of the new two-pay-cheque families also will create and support many good money-making job opportunities. As two-income families increase, people have the need and the income to spend heavily for personal services and labour-saving appliances, as well as for restaurant meals and leisure activities. These businesses will have many job openings for employees, for executives, and for people who want to go into business for themselves.

Help in choosing a career among the good new opportunities

There are around 1,000 Careers Offices throughout the UK, run by your local education authority. Although they are mainly there to advise school leavers and students, they will also help people returning to work after a break. They can also tell you about training opportunities and help you decide on a course to suit you. You can make an appointment to see the Careers Officer.

You can also get advice from the Employment Adviser in a job-centre, or make an appointment to see the TOPS Officer. TOPS is the Training Opportunities Scheme, run by the government, which offers courses lasting between one month and a year. Courses are free and some are held at business schools and colleges of further education. While training, you get a weekly allowance. It is normal practice that you have to take a skill test before you are accepted for a course.

Most cities have a Professional and Executive Recruitment (PER) office, which is largely to help people with qualifications or experience to find suitable managerial and executive jobs. They also organise seminars which give you advice on job-hunting, writing letters, filling in forms, and so on. The seminars are free to job-seekers.

If you want to get more details of these and other possibilities in training, get a booklet called *Fresh Start: A guide to training opportunities* from the Equal Opportunities Commission or from job-centres and employment offices. It is written especially for women who want a new, better paid, or more worthwhile job, whether it is just after school or after being out of the job market for some years.

Should I go back to college?

Returning to college full time or part time while you continue working is, of course, a good way to train or retrain for a promotion and/or an occupation that interests you. Be careful, though, not to squander time, effort, and energy training for jobs that do not exist. Also consider what the daily routine of an occupation is like before choosing it.

For example, one young woman spent years obtaining first a bachelor's and then a master's degree in biology. She enjoyed her studies, the classroom discussions. When she began work, she found herself alone most of the day in a laboratory and discovered she hated the kind of routine the job required. Another young woman graduated from college with a degree in photographic journalism. She found the field swamped with people from places with prestige departments in photo-journalism – and because of the glut of applicants no one would even give her an interview.

The essential ingredient in protecting yourself from studying for the wrong career or for a very overcrowded career requires that you do not rely too heavily on school job counsellors.

Though it is their job to help you choose your courses and your career goals, their advice is not always worthwhile. Despite their training and certification, not all employment counsellors are competent. One woman remembers having heard of a college programme where in five years instead of the usual four she could obtain both an engineering degree and a liberal arts degree in her other great interest, journalism. The counsellor insisted no such dual programme existed anywhere and that she would have to choose one or the other. When the young woman ignored the counsellor's advice and searched on her own, she found the dual programme did exist in a college only twenty miles away.

All of which means you can never blindly accept a counsellor's suggestions. You yourself must check out programmes in competing institutions. Furthermore, even a 100 per cent perfect counsellor cannot crawl inside your head and inside your emotions and advise you on whether you will be happy in a certain occupation. *No matter what occupation you're considering*, you should put personal effort into obtaining the relevant facts.

Talk to people who are now employed in that occupation and ask them to describe hour by hour a typical day's routine, a typical week's routine. Picture yourself doing that. Would you enjoy it? Many people, for example, devote 10 exhausting years of their lives to becoming doctors without ever considering whether they really want a lifetime daily routine of listening to anxious people talk about their problems. Others struggle to become professional popular singers or professional band instrumentalists without considering whether they want a life of living out of a suitcase as they travel from engagement to engagement.

Anything more I should know?

In the end, only you can determine your career opportunities. Anyone who has been out of college for a few years has noticed how varied are the careers of her peers. Yet, when they graduated, they started with almost the same qualifications.

Different people have different career goals. They seek and accept different types of jobs. Most don't try too hard and 'fall into' the first job that superficially satisfies them. Others, more adventurous and perceptive, determine their goals, then seek the job that will start them on their way. Next it becomes a matter of working hard, recognising opportunity when it comes along – and using your skills and wits to build on what you have.

Yes, luck helps. But by training for an expanding occupation, job-hunting where the jobs are, and working intelligently, you make your own luck.

PART VI

EPILOGUE

CHAPTER 29

The home front

Your man's attitude towards your job

Many men are now taking their two-career marriages very seriously. In a report in *Personnel Journal* an executive recruiter admits that 35 per cent of all male executive-job candidates will not accept a position in a new location unless it also meets their wives' job or study needs. Another research project concludes 'men with working wives are consistently less inclined to make long distance moves.' And *Business Week* lists 'dual-career marriage' first in a cover-article discussion of why workers are resisting relocation.

It also works in reverse, according to a *Wall Street Journal* report. Husbands nowadays relocate to follow their wives' career opportunities. The *Journal* even mentions two men who followed their executive wives all the way to the Middle East.

A criterion that many couples have found useful in making their decisions involves the kinds of work they do. For example, if the husband's skill is a generalised one and his wife's is highly specialised, his quitting to follow her may be the only sensible solution. A couple in which the man is a sales representative and the woman a marine biologist would be an example of his generalised skill and her specialised training. A good sales representative, after all, can find many excellent jobs in almost any community but there are relatively few locales where a marine biologist can find appropriate employment. Of course, if it's the man with the specialised skill and the woman with the general ability, then it's she who has to expect to relocate.

Before you adopt an unhealthy attitude of eternal gratitude to the man in your life for his liberated ideas, it's important to understand that men are getting a lot of rewards from the new two-career family arrangements. The values they're receiving are additional proof that women's liberation really does help *both* sexes. The man with a working wife usually learns to live on and need two incomes. If his wife cannot duplicate her job in the new town, it doesn't pay him to move. His new pay increase – without her income – will result in a lower standard of living for him. Furthermore, as liberation allows men to recognise the emotional part of their nature, many men are realising they themselves shrink from the upheaval of relocation, with its loss of family, friends, and familiar surroundings. The income from two careers in the family gives the man the freedom to follow his impulses and refuse the relocation offer.

Coping when both of you work

Almost half of all couples who are fighting rising prices with 'his' and 'her' jobs have to learn a new life style. When husbands and wives do adjust, a *Wall Street Journal* survey has found their marriages are better than ever.

Three of the most common difficulties are: changes in the husband-wife relationship, household chores, and child care. A woman with a job has direct access to money. This new feminine strength usually produces a subtle shift in the family power structure. The old dominant-husband, subservient-wife arrangement is replaced by a more equal relationship. Psychotherapist Rebecca Shephard says that in a two-job family, both men and women must realise there are emotions they must work through. The average man, she says, has a conflict between wanting his wife to remain dependent on him yet also not wanting to be tied down by her dependency. She, in turn, often wants the independence but is worried about his reactions. This can end in constant arguments about silly things such as the waste basket not being emptied or a towel not being replaced instead of dealing with the real anxieties. Says Dr Shephard, the husband needs to be willing to give up some of the control he is accustomed to and she needs to be willing to reassure him that he is still important to her.

Families who adjust also solve the demands of household chores and child care. They use the new increased income to buy household cleaning services, restaurant meals, and other time and energy savers and they revise their expectations. One survey by *Woman's Day* indicates job-holding women eliminate half or more of their former household chores. 'Time and human energy allow for just so much,' the women say. Men also recognise that they must assume housekeeping responsibilities because their wives are sharing the burden of supporting the family. Child care, too, becomes a joint mother/father undertaking. Instead of the old pattern of father going to work all day, coming home and being the disciplinarian, fathers are becoming part of their children's total daily life. James A. Levine, in his book *Who Will Raise the Children?* (Lippincott), reports that many men are finding enormous satisfaction in this newly expanded paternal role.

Choosing the right day care for your children

This is a rather ambitious heading, since we all know there's a terrible shortage of any kind of care facilities. Many couples just feel thankful if they can persuade somebody to take on the toddler.

Local authorities run day nurseries, but the demand for places means that 'in practice the children of two-parent families where both parents want or need to work or study are excluded'. The Department of Education runs nursery schools and classes, but they are only open between 9 am and 3.30 pm and are closed in school holidays. A few areas have opened extended-hours nursery schools, to cater for working parents, but again they close down in school holidays.

A newer development are childrens' centres, a kind of cross between day nurseries and nursery schools and these often act as a kind of focus and support for playgroups and other informal child-care. There are too few of them and administrative problems mean that it will take a while before they really get going.

Playgroups run by voluntary and community organisations are popular, but most are part-time. Some, however, do offer extended day care. These are supplemented by community nurseries, also run by voluntary community organisations. But (need we say it?) there are few of these.

Unless you work for a big enough organisation to make it worthwhile putting the pressure on to try and get a crèche or worksite day nursery, your only other option is a childminder. Childminding ranges from stimulating support to the child to really horrific neglect. Few minders register with their local authorities and it is very difficult to be sure which category the one you find will turn out to be. There is now a National Childminding Association, which will undoubtedly ensure some reasonable minimum standards and help parents to find their way to reliable minders.

Meanwhile, you have to face the fact that if you work and have pre-school children, you are going to have to spend a lot of time and effort in finding somebody to look after them. And a lot of money.

Solving your 'Superwoman' job-plus-home problems

A study of women's employment in Britain in the 1970s found that one-fifth of wives in paid employment neither had help from other members of the household, nor had any paid help.

The well-known feminist author, Betty Friedan, told a public meeting recently:

'We told our daughters you can have it all. Well, can they have it all? Only by being Superwoman. Well I say NO to Superwoman!'

'By any media calculation, the audience was a collection of superwomen. They wore their raised consciousness layered with dress-for-success suits. Yet they broke into spontaneous applause. They, too, were saying no to the Superwoman myth.'

Janice Conner dates one of the happiest changes in her family life to an evening when the apples in her kitchen fruit bowl began to show signs of shrivelling. As she and her husband sat drinking their after-dinner coffee, he glanced toward the bowl and said 'I've been watching those apples for 3 days. They should be in the refrigerator.' Automatically she put down her cup and was reaching for the bowl when something like the cartoonist's idea-bulb lit in her head. 'There's no lock on the refrigerator door,' she heard herself saying. 'It's your home. If you've known for 3 days that they ought to be in the refrigerator, why didn't you pick them up and put them there?'

'After I finished,' she says, 'we sat there stunned and stared at each other. I was as surprised by that idea as he was.'

In that admission of 'I was as surprised by that idea as he was,' Janice demolishes the popular complaint that women's job-plus-homemaking overload is the result of a male plot. 'If I didn't see it till that minute, why be furious with him because he didn't yet see it?'

Numerous large-scale surveys indicate that most women are as myopic as our friend. By and large, they neither receive nor *expect* significant homemaking effort from their men. The result, as Fran Litman, director for the Center for Parenting Studies at Boston's Wheelock College, has pointed out is that 'Too many women finish a whole day's work and then face a "second shift" at home.'

Elsewhere, at a Saturday night party a different angle of the managing-job-and-home problem surfaced. Five men were standing around discussing the daily hassles involved in bringing and fetching their children from day care. 'My wife said yesterday that if she didn't work, life wouldn't be so hectic,' said a bearded accountant. 'And I said to her, "What do you mean if you don't work? You *must* work! We need your pay-cheque. We can't manage without it!"'

The husband was echoing what economists have been pointing out for years. In today's inflationary economy, the wife in a two-pay-cheque family isn't being 'allowed' to work by her husband. He depends on her to help bring money into the family. Her income eases his financial anxieties and often frees him from the need to take on a second job. In short, with her pay they are buying not frills but the necessities of middle-class living. Economist Eliot Janeway credits women's income and the family buying power it provides with keeping families solvent amid inflation and with keeping the entire economy steady. Sylvia Porter puts it this way: 'Were it not for the double income, and I speak with great restraint, we would never have reached the living levels we have.'

However, like the woman with the apples who for so long did not see, *most women who help support their families do not yet understand the real meaning of their pay-cheque.* They don't see that if they have relieved their men of some of the traditional 'man's responsibility' to support the family, then logically the men *should* relieve them of some of the traditional 'woman's responsibility' for home and children.

The usual system of trying to get the man in the home to 'help' misses the solution completely and compounds the problem!

As most women who have tried it know, when you ask a man to help with homemaking, you have to coax and jolly him along and then be oh-so-constantly grateful. It makes for tension and exasperation and bickering for both of you.

The author of a woman's career book who collected the experiences of five hundred job-holding wives discovered that women who solved the 'help' problem also eliminated the family tension, exasperation, and bickering associated with it. In short, everybody's life was much pleasanter.

How did they solve it? Asking for aid always reinforced the outmoded idea that the home was 'her job'. In a situation where she was doing some of 'his' job of supporting the family, it made no sense to go on acting as if the home should be exclusively her responsibility. The women who made a family breakthrough eliminated the word and concept of *help* from their vocabulary. They shifted to 'We're both supporting our family. Now we have to figure out our other mutual job of how to take care of our home and family.'

One woman interviewed spoke for many when she

explained 'It's not just what my husband does. It's the reason he is doing it. He has taken over the weekly grocery shopping, several dinners a week, portions of the housecleaning and lots of child care. He's not helping me and he's not doing me a favour. After all, they're our children; it's our home; and doing something regularly about caring for them is now not only my job but his job too.'

These women's discovery that an altered family life style could be arrived at – *if they would but make the active effort to alter it* – is not unusual. Another study, a university project researching the problem, found that working wives who really believed in male-female equality had *happier marriages* than middle-of-the-road women who tried single-handedly to carry both the job and the homemaking responsibilities.

A mini-test used in the research spotlighted the women who 'really believed in equality'. The test asked 'If you were working, which solutions to home and career conflicts would you arrive at?' It then tells women to choose *as many* of the answers as seem appropriate.

Try it yourself. If you were working, would you solve problems by:

1. Trying to make it up to your husband.
2. Doing better on 'all fronts'.
3. Trying to separate home and work.
4. Expect your husband to accept less perfection at home.
5. Expect him to do more.
6. Expect him to see your problem of carrying both home and outside responsibilities.

Women who believe strongly in equality usually choose 4, 5, and 6, which require the husband to contribute to the family adjustment to the wife's home and career contributions. Choosing 1, 2, and 3, which depend entirely on the wife's efforts, indicates the woman *expects* her husband to stick to the old stereotypical male standards. Since that is her attitude on the subject, she inevitably conveys her beliefs to her husband. His behaviour then in part at least reflects *her* expectation that he *shouldn't* contribute to home maintenance or child-nurturing.

After studying all the data, the sociologist researcher Dr Catherine Arnott wrote of the equality-minded wives: 'Their success in developing a cooperative attitude from their husbands seemed to be the result of the wives' willingness to talk conflict out rather than trying to work around the problems. In short, they often lived up to their husbands' expectations by *changing the men's standards. The liberal wives' belief that their husbands should be willing to contribute to the family adjustment seems to make the couple skilful at hammering out innovative relationships.* And the husbands often respond with pride in their wives' accomplishments and individuality.'

Another ongoing study by Bernard Flicker of the City University of New York on the effect of woman's liberation on men comes to many of the same conclusions. Dr Flicker explains that husbands seem to alter their attitudes and behaviour and take on family responsibilities *when their wives expect them to and actively insist on it.* It is the *active role* of the woman talking up and 'educating' her husband to the new two-pay-cheque family life style that seems to be the key to whether or not he alters his behaviour, says Dr Flicker. The actual words each wife uses differ, but her meaning is the same: 'I have taken over some of your job of supporting this family. Now you must take over some of the job of maintaining our home and caring for our children.'

Therefore the 1980s' answer to the 1970s' question of 'How will she manage a job and a family?' is:

She won't manage. She and he together will manage.

But we women must ourselves first understand that we must abandon our passive stance of waiting for him to share the responsibilities; we must abandon talking in terms of being 'helped' because it reinforces the outmoded idea that home and children are exclusively women's jobs. *We* must instead, as Dr Flicker puts it, 'actively insist' on our men assuming *responsibility* for home and children – just as women are assuming responsibility for supporting the family. Only when we women ourselves comprehend this can we say the things in reasonable words and actions that will help our men and children understand it – and live it.

Index